BASIC FILM-MAKING

ARCO FILM SERIES

BASIC FILM-MAKING

DANA H. HODGDON
STUART M. KAMINSKY

ARCO PUBLISHING, INC.
NEW YORK

Published by Arco Publishing, Inc.
219 Park Avenue South, New York, N.Y. 10003

Library of Congress Cataloging in Publication Data

Hodgdon, Dana H.
   Basic filmmaking.
   Includes index.
    1. Cinematography.   I. Kaminsky, Stuart M.
II. Title.
TR850.H57   778.5'3   81–613
ISBN 0–668–05148–5 (Cloth Edition)   AACR2
ISBN 0–668–05156–6 (Paper Edition)

Printed in the United States of America

Illustrations . . . . .Katherine Blind
Photographs . . . . .Erik Wiklund
Acknowledgments . . . . .Steven Wystrach, Steven Fagin,
Ray Narducy, Hap Kindem

Contents

BASIC FILM-MAKING

Basic Technology

A logical starting point in the study of filmmaking is to discuss the basic technology of how motion pictures work. This involves several areas: the theory of the celluloid moving image, the various film formats which are the primary medium of filmmaking, the motion picture camera, and exposure, the process whereby light is converted into images on film. These four elements of motion picture technology will be the subject matter of the first chapter of this text.

The Moving Image

Filmmaking is a combination of writing, music, graphic arts, acting and a very sophisticated technology which has made sound, color and widescreen possible. Every film or motion picture ever produced, from *The Birth of a Nation* to *Heaven's Gate* to the newsfilm portions on the six o'clock news, is based on a simple truth: in fact, the movies do not move at all. A strip of motion picture film contains no motion whatsoever. This strip of film is made up of a series of still pictures or *frames* which are exposed one at a time in the camera and projected one at a time in the projector. Motion, or to be more precise, the illusion of motion, is perceived by the viewer because of the complex way in which film images are recorded in the camera and projected onto a screen, and because the viewer's mind and eye, working together, perceive motion in a series of still pictures projected in rapid succession.

The illusion of motion is directly related to human visual perception. This illusion is based on a phenomenon known as the *persistence of vision.*

This simply means that in the perception process, the eye and brain retain light images for a fraction of a second. Thus, if one moves a burning sparkler in a circular motion in a darkened room, the human eye "sees" a circle of light rather than the pinpoint of light emitted by the sparkler. The faster the sparkler is moved, the more the eyes and mind tend to "see" it as a constant line or circle. This phenomenon, the persistence of vision, is the principle upon which the technology of the motion picture is based. Thus, still pictures projected rapidly and sequentially give the illusion of motion. A strip of motion picture film, delineating some action, is actually a series of still pictures in a sequence. The action is broken into still images, usually 24 still images per second when filmed in the camera or projected on the screen.

The process in the camera works as follows (Fig. 1-1):

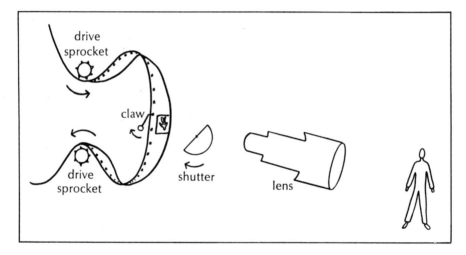

Fig. 1-1. The camera transport mechanism.

The claw engages in a sprocket hole and pulls a frame of film into place for exposure. During this process, the shutter is closed. When the film is in place, the shutter opens and a frame is exposed to light for approximately 1/50th of a second (this depends on transport speed, to be discussed later in this chapter). After the exposure has been made, the shutter closes, the claw engages another sprocket hole and the process starts over. For projection, the process is the same except that an image is projected rather than recorded (Fig. 1-2). The claw pulls an image into place for projection and during this time, the shutter is closed. When the single frame is in position in the gate area, the shutter opens and the image is projected onto the screen for approximately 1/50th of a second. Then the shutter closes, the new frame is pulled into place and the cycle continues. In the projection process, the eyes and mind retain the image of one frame while the screen is black and the next frame is being pulled into place. Thus, the rapid, sequential projection of still pictures results in an illusion of motion—the moving picture.

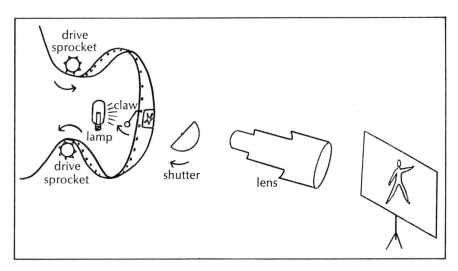

Fig. 1-2. The projection transport mechanism.

Most films are photographed and projected at the rate of 24 frames per second (fps). This is true for most sound films and is, therefore, sometimes called "sound speed." Many early silent films, such as the films of Charlie Chaplin and Buster Keaton, were filmed at a variety of speeds and usually projected at 16 fps. As a result, 16 fps has become known as "silent speed." Most silent Super-8 and regular 8mm films are shot and projected at 18 fps. The illusion of motion can be maintained at this transport speed and less film is used when shooting at 18 fps:

10 seconds of action shot at 18 fps = 180 frames of film

10 seconds of action shot at 24 fps = 240 frames of film

So, 25 percent less film is used for a given shot when shooting at 18 fps rather than 24 fps.

Slow motion results when film is shot at a higher speed that it is projected. Thus, an action recorded at 48 fps and projected at 24 fps will be perceived as slow motion. The 48 frames of film representing one second of action will take two seconds at 24 fps to travel through the projector. Conversely, fast motion results when an action is filmed at a slower transport speed than it is projected. When a shot is photographed at 12 fps and projected at 24 fps, fast or speeded-up motion will result.

Formats

Since its inception in the late nineteenth century, the motion picture has evolved into a variety of formats, suitable for a variety of uses and applications. This evolutionary process began over 80 years ago, and has included the rise and fall of a great variety of film widths and gauges. Today, there are only five (actually four, as will be discussed below) standard and widely used film formats.

70mm. The 70mm film format is the largest and most expensive film gauge in use. It is the film type used for some high budget Hollywood features. Examples of films shot in 70mm are *Around the World in 80 Days, Star, The Wind and the Lion* and *Ryan's Daughter.* The 70mm format offers two possibilities for theatrical distribution. For some large, exclusive, big city theaters, films shot in 70mm are distributed in 70mm. For general distribution in neighborhood theaters, these 70mm films are reduced on an optical printer and distributed in 35mm.

The great advantage of 70mm is in the image quality. The color and sharpness of films shot in 70mm are unsurpassed by any other film format. The great disadvantage is in cost. It is the most expensive type of film to shoot. It is, therefore, a format which is used only for very high budget feature films. Recent rises in the cost of film materials have made the 70mm format virtually obsolete.

35mm. The 35mm gauge is the standard format for most feature films, most television series (which are shot on film rather than videotape), and most television commercials (also not on videotape). 35mm is also a standard format for motion picture theaters, as almost all film theaters use 35mm projectors. The 35mm format is very expensive and, therefore, beyond the realm of possibility for independent and low budget filmmakers. The budgets for feature films are very high—usually 5–10 million dollars. Both *Apocalypse Now* and *The Blues Brothers* cost in excess of 40 million dollars to produce.

It is obvious that for low budget filmmaking 35mm is not the format.

16mm. The 16mm format has a great many applications and uses. Industrial films, educational films, documentaries and some television commercials are all shot in 16mm. Furthermore, several low budget feature films, like *Faces* and *The Endless Summer*, as well as feature documentaries like *Woodstock, High School, Gimme Shelter* and *I.F. Stone's Weekly*, have been shot in 16mm. Shooting in 16mm costs less than half as much as shooting in 35mm. Because of this, 16mm is the most widely used format in advanced film courses in colleges and universities.

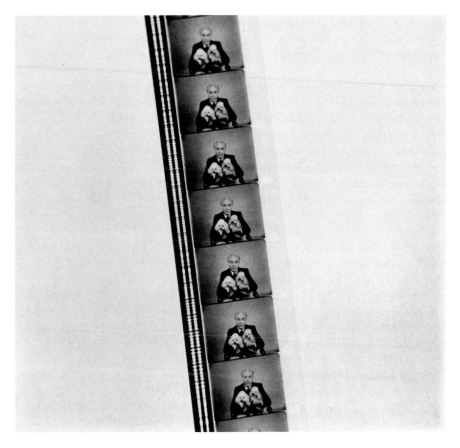

16mm film with optical soundtrack along non-sprocketed edge.

For the independent filmmaker, 16mm offers the advantage of portable, lightweight equipment and relatively inexpensive film stock and lab costs. However, the complexity of 16mm equipment and the costs of this equipment with film stock and processing, makes 16mm a format better suited to the advanced independent filmmaker, rather than the beginning one.

Therefore, in reference to the above-mentioned formats: the larger the format or film size, the higher the quality of the film images when projected on a screen. But the larger the format, the more expensive that format will be to work in.

Beginning filmmaking efforts are usually undertaken utilizing a film size which is some variation of the 8mm format. This includes regular 8mm, Super-8 and single 8mm. These are the least expensive of all film formats in which to work. Unfortunately, they also render the lowest quality film images of all widely used formats. All three of these formats use film that is 8mm wide (approximately ¼-inch). Yet, all three are slightly different from one another and, except for special cases, are not interchangeable.

Regular 8mm (sometimes called Double-8 or simply, 8mm). This format first became popular in the 1930s as an amateur format based on the 16mm format. Regular 8mm film is simply 16mm film with twice the number of sprocket holes. The regular 8mm frame is approximately one half as high and wide as the 16mm frame. The 16mm film, with the extra sprocket holes, is run through the regular 8mm camera on two passes. The first pass exposes one side of the film and the second pass exposes the other side. The film is then processed by the lab and slit down the middle and spliced together on a single reel.

Super-8. This format was first introduced in 1965 as a replacement for regular 8mm. It features smaller sprocket holes and a smaller distance between frames. The result is a larger frame area, some 50 percent larger, and this means a higher quality image than regular 8mm. Super-8 film comes pre-loaded in a sealed cartridge. Loading a Super-8 camera is simply a matter of snapping the cartridge into the camera—no threading is necessary. Unloading the camera is just as simple.

Single 8mm. The single 8mm format is exactly the same as Super-8 in size, sprocket holes and image area. However, the cartridges for single 8mm are manufactured by Fujica of Japan and are considerably different in design than the conventional cartridge used in Super-8. The single 8mm cartridge must be used in a Fujica camera, the only camera designed to accept the single 8mm cartridge.

Choosing between Regular 8mm, Super-8 and Single 8mm. Regular 8mm equipment is no longer being manufactured, although a variety of film stocks are still offered for it. Used regular 8mm cameras and projectors are available at good prices at camera stores and through private owners. A disadvantage to regular 8mm, of course, is that the cameras must be loaded twice for each roll of film; two passes of the 25-foot double 8mm roll are made through the camera before the film is processed and slit. The Super-8 format offers the widest variety and availability of equipment, accessories, film stocks and services. Super-8 cameras are available in price ranges from $100 to $1500. The cartridge loading feature makes for quick and easy loading. The disadvantage lies in the fact that some special effects possible in regular 8mm and single 8mm are not possible in Super-8 because of the cartridge design. There is no back wind capability on most Super-8 cameras, although some expensive Super-8 cameras

Super-8mm and regular 8mm film.

have limited back wind features. Hence, no in-camera dissolves or super-impositions are possible on most Super-8 cameras. More about this in a later chapter.

Single 8mm, being a Fujica system, is limited to films and cameras offered by Fujica. Super-8 projectors and viewers are compatible with single 8mm film. The Fujica cartridge design is such that easy back winding is possible. In conjunction with this, several single 8mm cameras in the Fujica line have dissolve and superimposition features.

In summary, Super-8 now has a near monopoly on the amateur market and is being experimented with in television news and documentaries. It offers cameras and accessories incorporating the latest technological developments. Super-8 film, marketed by Kodak and others, offers the latest developments in image quality and film sensitivity. The Super-8 format is, therefore, usually a first choice for beginning, low budget filmmaking.

Cameras

The basic tool in filmmaking, regardless of the format, is the motion picture camera. The camera can be an extension of the imagination or it can ruin a filmmaking effort from the outset. The difference in what it can do lies in how well it is understood and therefore, how effectively it can be applied to the filmmaking process.

Basically, all cameras must photograph a series of still pictures in rapid succession, 18 fps for silent films and 24 fps for sound films. To achieve this, all cameras have a *transport mechanism*. This transport mechanism consists of: a window (called the gate) in which each frame is exposed to light coming through the lens; a shutter, which opens and closes in front of the lens; a claw, which engages the film in the sprocket holes and pulls the film into place for exposure. As described earlier in this chapter, the gate, shutter and claw combine to expose still photographs at the rate determined by the transport speed. These elements comprise what is called the registration-transport system of the camera. There are several other basic components of all motion picture cameras:

Viewing Systems. One of the most important features of any camera is its viewing system. This is the system in the camera that enables the cameraperson to view, frame and focus what is being filmed. Basically, there are two types—view finder viewing systems and reflex viewing systems. View finder systems use an auxiliary lens or finder to simulate for the eye what is being seen by the filming lens. Reflex systems permit viewing through the filming lens. View finder systems are found in old regular 8mm cameras and some less expensive Super-8 and 16mm cameras. The primary disadvantage of the view finder system is that the focusing and framing are not exact. This is because what is seen through the view finder is not what is being recorded on the film. Focusing must be estimated or tape measured and set by the footage numbers on the lens. The view finder system creates a problem called parallax. Parallax is the slight difference in framing between what is seen by the view finder lens and the filming lens. Some cameras have a parallax adjustment, so that when focus is set on the filming lens, the parallax must be adjusted on the view finder.

Reflex viewing systems are a standard feature on most medium-priced and expensive Super-8 cameras. Most reflex viewing systems work on a beam splitter system or a prism system, both of which are similar. The beam splitter is a glass wedge in the rear of the lens which directs approximately 10 percent of the light to the viewing system and 90 percent of the light to the film plane. Thus the reflex system permits viewing of what is going onto the film.

The diopter adjustment on the eyepiece of the Canon 814 camera. The open-close switch is for opening and closing the viewfinder.

Nearly all reflex cameras have a provision for making diopter adjustments. The diopter adjusts the reflex viewing system to the eye of the cameraperson. Having the diopter set correctly makes focusing the lens easier and means that the cameraperson does not have to wear glasses, if he or she normally wears glasses. The diopter can be set correctly in the following way:

The camera is pointed at something extremely far away. The horizon is usually best. The lens focus ring is set on infinity. The diopter is adjusted by the naked eye—no glasses should be worn. The diopter adjustment is usually a screw or knob located near the eye cup of the camera. When what is seen through the lens is as sharp as it can be, the diopter is adjusted properly for the eye of the cameraperson for any kind of shooting with that camera. If someone else is to use the camera, the diopter must be re-set to that person's vision.

Lenses. The camera lens, when it is understood and appreciated, can be one of the most creative tools in filmmaking. All lenses are classified according to their focal length. This refers to the enlarging or magnifying power of the lens. Lenses are manufactured in a variety of focal lengths and are usually classified as wide angle, normal and telephoto lenses. The normal lens is a lens that accepts an angle of view approximately 22 or 23 degrees horizontally. A wide angle lens accepts a very wide field of view and makes things seem farther away. A telephoto lens accepts a narrow angle of view and makes things seem closer to the camera. The focal lengths which correspond to wide angle, normal and telephoto vary according to the format. In 16mm:

Wide angle	15mm or lower
Normal	25mm
Telephoto	45mm or higher

In Super-8, regular 8mm and single 8mm:

Wide angle	9mm or lower
Normal	12mm
Telephoto	25mm or higher

A certain focal length lens determines not only image size, but perspective and depth of field as well. Perspective refers to spatial relationships of near and far objects. For example, a shot consists of an actor standing 10 feet in front of a house and the camera is 10 feet in front of the actor. If a normal lens is selected for this shot, the perspective of the scene will be rendered naturally. All relationships will appear the same on the film in two dimensions as they did in the actual three dimensional situation. However, if the scene is shot with a wide angle lens, the perspective will be changed. Not only will the actor appear to be farther away from the camera, but the house will appear to be more than 10 feet from the actor. If the same scene is shot with a telephoto lens, the change in perspective will be reversed. The actor will appear closer to the camera and the house will appear closer to the actor. Generally speaking, wide angle lenses exaggerate the distance between objects. The shorter the focal length of the lens being used, the greater this exaggeration. Telephoto lenses compress the distance between objects on different planes. There will be a more detailed discussion of the uses of wide angle and telephoto lenses in a later chapter.

Depth of field refers to the nearest and farthest points from the camera in a particular shot which will be in focus. From the preceding example, the lens is focused on the actor standing in front of the house and therefore, the lens focus ring is set at 10 feet because the camera is 10 feet from the actor. The depth of field in this shot might be 5–20 feet; that is, everything between 5 feet in front of the camera and 20 feet away from the camera will be sharply in focus. Things outside that range, either closer or farther away, will be out of focus. Three factors determine depth of field. These are f-stop (which will be discussed later), the focal length of the lens and the distance from the camera to the subject.

A general rule is this: telephoto lenses (in Super-8, lenses of 25mm or more) create a shallow depth of field, wide angle lenses (in Super-8, 8mm or less) create a large depth of field. High f-stop numbers (11, 16, 22) render a great depth of field, low f-stop numbers render a shallow depth of field. The greater the distance between subject and camera, the greater the depth of field. And the closer the subject is to the camera, the shallower the depth of field. These are functions of lens design and apply to all lenses. The principles of perspective and depth of field, as well as image size, should be considered in choosing a lens for a given shot. Usually a medium shot (one person and the immediate surroundings) is filmed with a normal lens. An establishing shot, such as the opening shots in most westerns, is captured with a wide angle lens. For a close-up, such as a close-up of someone's watch or a telephone, a telephoto lens is used. Close-ups of people are most visually pleasing when shot with a telephoto lens. Normal lenses tend to make people look a little chubby and weak chinned. Telephoto lenses tend to make people's faces look more angular and stronger. The ideal portrait lens is between 40mm and 60mm in 16mm, and in Super-8 between 20mm and 30mm.

Zoom lenses, which are discussed later in this text, are simply variable

An extreme wide angle lens can cause distortion because it exaggerates distances.

The same framing with a wide angle, normal and telephoto lens. The background behind the subject appears smaller and farther away with the wide angle lens and closer and larger with the normal and telephoto lens. Normal lens.

Wide angle lens.

Telephoto lens.

focal length lenses. They are classified according to the range of focal lengths they cover. A standard in 16mm filming is the Angenieux 12–120mm zoom lens. This lens can be set at any focal length between 12mm and 120mm. It covers a full range of wide angle, normal and telephoto focal lengths. This lens is also referred to as a 10:1 zoom lens. It has a variable focal length ratio of 10:1. Most Super-8 cameras are marketed with zoom lenses. These are generally 5:1 zoom lenses (9mm–45mm) in the mid-price range and 6:1, 8:1 or 10:1 in the higher price ranges.

A Note on Focusing. The lens should always be focused on the principal or most important part of a shot. Proper focus will be maintained as long as the subject-to-camera distance remains the same. If that distance should change because the subject moves closer or farther away from the camera, the focus setting on the lens should be adjusted accordingly. The lens focus must be changed during a shot if the camera pans from one subject to another and the two subjects are different distances from the camera. This is called *pulling* or *racking* (Fig. 1-3). If a shot calls for a pan from one actor who is 5 feet from the camera to another actor who is 10 feet from the camera, the focus ring must be turned during the pan from 5 feet to 10 feet. A camera assistant is usually designated as the

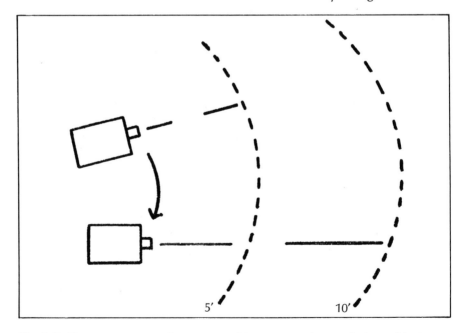

Fig. 1-3. The camera pans from one subject to another and the subjects are different distances from the camera. Focus must be "pulled" from five feet to ten feet.

focus puller. The assistant turns the focus ring on the camera from one distance to another during the pan while the cameraperson executes the pan and concentrates on proper framing and movement. Focus and focus pulling can be used for emphasis. For example, different planes of focus can be exploited in the following shot:

A telephone is framed in the extreme foreground of the shot, 5 feet from the camera. Ten feet from the camera, in the background of the shot, there is a person sitting. A relationship between the telephone and the person is established by starting the shot with the lens focused at 5 feet and then, during the shot, changing the focus to 10 feet. At the beginning of the shot, the telephone will be in focus and the person in the background will be out of focus and indistinguishable. By the end of the shot, the telephone will be out of focus and the person will be sharply defined and in focus.

The proper procedure for focusing a zoom lens is:

Zoom the lens *in* (to the telephoto or close-up position) to the primary subject. Focus the lens on that subject. Zoom out to the desired framing. The subject will remain in focus as long as the same subject-to-camera distance is maintained. When a new shot is set up with a new subject-to-camera distance, the same procedure must be followed. Zoom in, focus the lens and zoom out to the desired framing.

Exposure

The final section in this introductory chapter deals with the exposure of the film image. Most modern Super-8 cameras and even some 16mm cameras have built-in automatic exposure systems. This means that the camera will take care of this vital consideration. However, controlling exposure can be a creative tool in filmmaking. There may be times when it will be desirable to override the automatic exposure system on the camera and make subjective decisions regarding what is deemed to be the best exposure for a given shot. An automatic exposure meter cannot make creative decisions. In order to fully understand exposure, let us start at the beginning.

There are three factors which can be controlled and manipulated to change exposure. These factors are film speed or ASA, f-stop, and transport speed.

Film Speed (ASA). Film speed refers to the degree of sensitivity of the film to light. This sensitivity is designated by a number which is called the

The telephone is in focus; the person in the background is out of focus.

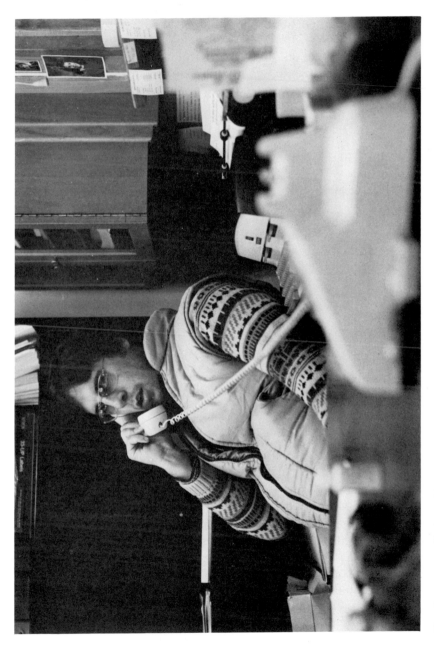

The focus is "pulled" to bring the person into sharp focus.

ASA. The higher the ASA number of the film, the more sensitive to light the film is. Thus, a film with a high ASA would be used in an indoor or low light shooting situation. Conversely, a film with a low number ASA (a film that is less sensitive to light) would be used in an outdoor setting. The following film stocks are the most widely used in Super-8 filmmaking:

FILM	ASA	TYPE
Slow Speed Films		
Fujichrome R25	25	D
Kodachrome 40	40/25	A
Ektachrome 40	40/25	A
GAF color	40/25	A
Plus-X	50/40	B&W
Fujichrome RT50	50/32	A
Medium Speed Films		
Ektachrome EF	125/80	B
Ektachrome 160	160/100	A
Ektachrome G	160	G
Ektachrome SM	160/100	B
Tri-X	200/160	B&W
Very Fast Films		
4-X	400/320	B&W
GAF 500	500	B&W

One might now ask, why not simply use a high speed film (like Tri-X ASA 200/160) all the time to make it possible to shoot freely both indoors and outdoors. The answer to this question is to be found in an analysis of the basic properties of film stocks. In general, faster films, films with a high ASA, are grainier and have less contrast than slower, low ASA film stocks. Therefore, fast films will look a bit less sharply focused and a little flatter than slow films. So what is gained in film sensitivity is lost in image quality. It is always a good idea to match a film stock to a shooting situation. Tri-X, Four-X or Ektrachrome 160 should not be used outdoors when better results could be achieved with Plus-X or Kodachrome 40. But Plus-X or Kodachrome 40 should be used indoors if there is enough light or enough light can be created. These two slower films will always make for better images than their faster counterparts if there is enough light.

In Super-8, the film cartridges are notched according to the ASA of the film contained. The notches relay the ASA of the film to a lever inside the magazine compartment of the camera. This device then "tells" the automatic meter what the speed of the film is. On regular 8mm cameras, the

ASA must be set by way of a dial on the camera. Some older Super-8 cameras do not have a metering system which can accept the faster films, Tri-X, Four-X and Ektachrome 160. The camera manual should be consulted to determine if this is the case.

In all cameras, the ASA ceases to be a variable once the camera has been loaded. The choice of film sensitivity and film quality has been made. Now two other factors must be considered.

Transport Speed. We mentioned transport speed earlier in this section. Standard silent speed in Super 8 is 18 fps and sound speed is 24 fps. Many Super-8 sound cameras can shoot and record sound at 18 fps with a certain loss of sound quality. If the film is to be a "silent" film in the film sense of the term (that is, a film which will never have a sound track physically combined with it), then shoot at 18 fps. In this way, the film is shot at silent speed and then projected with an accompanying sound track on a casette or ¼-inch player. If a sound track is to be added to the film by way of a magnetic stripe on the film, the original footage can be shot at either 24 fps or 18 fps.

In terms of exposure, transport speed has this effect: the faster the film is moving through the camera, the less light each individual frame will receive. The opposite holds true for fast motion (slow transport speed) shooting. A change in the transport speed results in a change in *shutter speed*. Shutter speed is the amount of time each frame is exposed to light. Usually the shutter speed is 1/36th of a second for silent speed filming and 1/48th of a second for filming at 24 fps. This means that each frame is exposed to light for 1/36th or 1/48th of a second. If the transport speed is 48 fps, the shutter speed is 1/96th of a second. In other words, less light hits each frame at this higher transport speed.

All cameras with automatic light meters make an internal automatic adjustment when transport speed is changed, so exposure remains constant and correct.

F-Stop. The f-stop on the camera is the internal iris device in the lens which regulates the amount of light coming to the film plane. It works very much like the pupil in the human eye which opens and closes in response to bright light or darkness. Effectively, this f-stop, or aperture as it is sometimes called, is the only variable in achieving proper exposure on a motion picture camera. The film speed (ASA) is fixed when the camera is loaded and the automatic meter "knows" the ASA by way of the notches on the film cartridge. The shutter speed is fixed when a transport speed is chosen and the meter automatically knows this. To achieve proper exposure, the meter automatically adjusts the f-stop iris according to the two factors just mentioned, which it "knows," and according to the ultimate variable—the light it reads in the scene which is being filmed. The iris closes down to a pinhole in bright shooting situations and opens up to let more light through to the film plane under low light conditions.

The degree to which the iris is opened or closed is defined in terms of numbers called f-stop numbers or simply f-stops (Fig. 1-4). These numbers can sometimes be confusing. All lenses have them. They simply refer to the opening of the iris. The f-stops are 1.4, 2, 2.8, 4, 5.6, 8, 11, 16, and 22. The larger the f-stop number, the smaller the amount of light let in through the lens. The smaller the f-stop number, the more light let in through the lens. The difference between one number and another is refered to as "one stop." One can also speak of ½ stop or ⅓ stop, etc. In speaking of f-stops, one speaks of opening up, that is letting more light in, or stopping down, meaning letting less light onto the film plane.

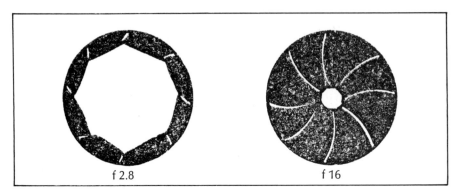

Fig. 1-4. The iris in the lens which determines f-stops.

Not all lenses have the same lowest f-stop number. Some lenses are able to let in more light than others. Therefore, some lenses are better for low light shooting than others. The lowest or minimum f-stop that a lens can open up to is usually engraved on the barrel of the lens along with the focal length of the lens or variable focal length in the case of a zoom lens. A lens on a Super-8 camera might be engraved with 7.5-60mm 1:1.4.

The f-stop control on the lens is tied into the automatic metering system of the camera. On many Super-8 and regular 8mm cameras, the f-stop meters are visible in the viewfinder of the camera. A needle points at the f-stop number that the automatic meter has chosen for a given scene. On some Super-8 cameras, the automatic control of the needle can be changed or overridden. This is done to darken or lighten a scene. To do this, the metering system of the camera must be changed from automatic to manual. The desired f-stop is selected by turning the appropriate dial

The zoom lens on the Canon 814 camera.

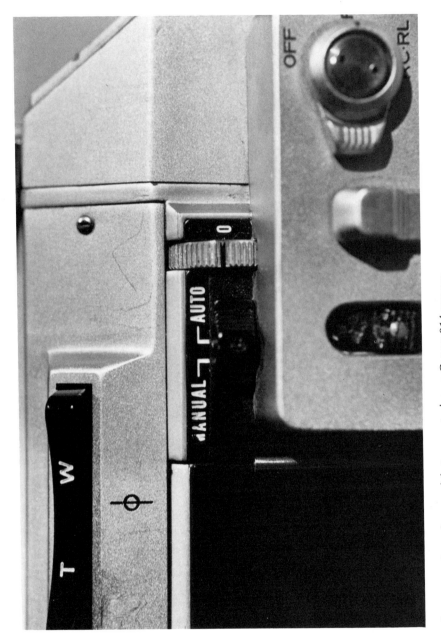

The automatic and manual f-stop control on a Canon 814 camera.

and lining the needle in the viewfinder opposite the f-stop number. Overriding the automatic exposure system can be accomplished as follows:

> With the meter on automatic, observe the f-stop number chosen by the automatic system. If the scene is to be darkened slightly, then reset the needle manually ½ to 1 stop higher in number (less light) than the number chosen by the automatic system. To darken a scene drastically, change the needle 1 to 1½ stops higher in number. Do the opposite to lighten a shot.

Be careful in overriding the automatic exposure system. To override means essentially to underexpose or overexpose the shot. This under- or overexposure may look like a technical error rather than creative control for the exposure of the shot. Be particularly careful when choosing to lighten a scene. Do not readjust the f-stop any further than one number. Otherwise, the scene will "wash out."

Usually one would choose to override the meter in a backlit lighting situation. This is where a light (the sun, if the shot is outdoors, or a light or window, if it is indoors) is directly behind the subject. In this kind of situation, the automatic meter will tend to expose for the backlight and therefore, underexpose for the subject. To override here by opening up half an f-stop (going toward a smaller number) would mean to improve the exposure on the subject's face. In this situation, it may sometimes be desirable to silhouette the subject's face, that is, darken the subject against the back light. To do this, "stop down" (go to a larger number) by 1 to 2 stops when overriding. In order to discover the exact consequences of overriding on a camera, it is wisest to experiment and do tests. The explanations provided above are to be used as guidelines only.

Another procedure to follow in a back-lit or dark background situation is as follows: walk up to your subject and frame only the subject's face in the viewfinder. Doing this means that the in-camera meter will read only the subject's face and not be "fooled" by the background. Observe the f-stop number chosen by the meter for the subject's face and override the meter to lock in at this f-stop. Then step back and frame the shot including the background. Exposure will be correct for the subject's face.

A change in f-stop number does more than change the amount of light striking the film. It also affects the depth of field, as mentioned earlier in the explanation of depth of field and focal length. Again, there is a simple rule: the larger the f-stop number, the greater the depth of field, and the smaller the f-stop number, the shallower the depth of field. Quite simply then, where there is a lot of light, outdoors or in very bright interiors, the meter will choose a high f-stop number and the depth of field will be great. In low light shooting situations, depth of field will be shallow as a

A backlit situation. The automatic in-camera meter has exposed for the background and the subject's face is underexposed.

result of the low f-stop number needed for proper exposure. As an extension of this, one can generalize and say that focus is less critical when shooting outdoors than when shooting indoors because of the f-stop differences and resulting differences in depth of field. Where there is a large depth of field, there is focus leeway and room for error. Where there is a shallow depth of field, the room for error is consideraly smaller and there is a greater possibility of having shots out of focus. Of course, the focal length of the lens and the subject-to-camera distance remain as factors affecting depth of field and should be considered along with f-stop.

This first chapter has been an introduction to the fundamentals of motion picture technology. In the following chapters, this technology will be applied to the theories and techniques of filmmaking.

2 Scriptwriting and Pre-Production

In learning and applying technology to filmmaking projects one must observe certain *rules*; there are certain technological absolutes that must be followed. For example, if the available light level for a given shot is too low (as indicated by the in-camera light meter), the film will be underexposed. This is a rule. Rules that apply to technology can and will evolve as new technologies for making motion pictures develop. The recent development of fast films and available light lenses (both developed over the past thirty years) have made for changes in the rules. An available light scene which was impossible to record with color film in 1950 may now be possible to record in color because of advancements in technology.

However, with virtually all other aspects of filmmaking there are no rules. Instead there are principles or *conventions*. For example, it is a convention in film that a fade out/fade in indicates elapsed time. This means that audiences will usually interpret a fade out/fade in as meaning that there has been some elapsed time between scenes. But this does not mean that this convention, when used, must mean elapsed time, nor does it mean that audiences will always interpret it as such. To use another example, twenty years ago it was a convention in feature films and broadcast television that it was wrong to let the light flares, produced when the lens is pointed into a direct light source (a light or the sun etc.), be part of a scene. Yet today, such lens flares are very common and are often considered arty.

In summary, rules are absolutes which apply to technology. As technology changes rules will change. Conventions (or principles, as sometimes referred to in this text) are generally accepted patterns, ways, or methods for communicating. Conventions have emerged and evolved throughout the history of motion pictures as writers, producers, directors, and editors have created and developed means for audiences to recognize and understand what is being communicated. Conventions too will change, as indicated in the lens flare example. So, one must follow the rules for the technology, equipment, film stocks, etc., with which one is working. And one can either work with, work around, or work against conventions, depending on how and what one wants to communicate.

Any filmmaking venture, whether it be a fiction film, a documentary film or an experimental film, involves essentially three stages. These are the pre-production stage, the production stage and the post-production stage. Generally speaking, the pre-production part of the filmmaking process involves the creation of the film script and the necessary planning that goes into preparing the script for shooting. The production stage involves the actual shooting of the film. The third stage, post-production, entails lab processing, editing and the preparation of the sound track and titles. These three stages should never be considered separate and distinct from one another. In fact, as will be emphasized throughout this text, the three must be thought of simultaneously. Successful filmmaking is often the result of thought and planning which involves the integration of the scripting of shots, the filming of these shots, and the editing of these shots. When these three stages are considered separately, when a film is scripted with little or no concern for shooting set-ups and possible problems or for the way in which shots will be cut together in the editing room, the results are usually poor in quality. While the subject of this chapter is this first stage of the filmmaking process, the filmmaker should always be thinking of the other two phases while scripting and planning a production.

Modes of Film

As will be mentioned often throughout this chapter, there are traditionally three modes or types of films. These are the narrative fiction film, the documentary film and the experimental film. Most films and film ideas are classified according to one or more of these modes. It is important in developing a film idea, to understand something about the history and conventions of each of these three modes and their possible combinations. This will aid in an understanding of audience expectations for various types of films and the conventions of these types of films (and therefore, how to experiment with these conventions). The following is a discussion of the various modes of film and the history, conventions and form of each mode.

Documentary. Documentary films, or films about "real" as opposed to "fictional" events, are not necessarily based on reality, but on convincing the audience of the reality of what they are seeing. It is the illusion of reality that counts. The filmmaker cannot simply capture reality, but he or she can present an ordered approximation of what he or she thinks reality is. In other words, documentary film often acts as a substitute for the audience's experiencing real events, through the filmmaker's eyes.

There are three different kinds of documentaries, three ways of convincing an audience that what they are seeing is "real." First, there is the re-enactment documentary. In such films, among the oldest of documentaries, the director has the people who experience something re-enact it for the camera. *Nanook of the North*, often considered the first documentary feature, was made in 1920–21 by Robert Flaherty. Flaherty lived with an Eskimo and had him re-enact scenes from his daily life, which he put together in a story about the difficulties of the life of an Eskimo. Flaherty created the illusion of reality by using real Eskimos, actual arctic locations, and authoritative statements of the truth of what was being seen, along with maps of the arctic area.

Flaherty's films like *Nanook, Moana, Man of Aran* and *Louisiana Story*, all make use of these devices. Furthermore, Flaherty uses two important techniques to convince the audience that what they are seeing is actually taking place. First, Flaherty uses long takes. He lets the camera run for as long as two or more minutes to allow an action to continue. To cut away from an action is to acknowledge that the action is staged. Flaherty staged the action, but used long takes to create the illusion that he was not staging. Second, Flaherty frequently photographed in depth. This simply means that he utilized the principles of depth of field. Because things in the foreground and further back in the image could be in focus, Flaherty frequently combined the long take with action in depth to give the illusion of things taking place spontaneously.

The second type of documentary is the social reconstruction documentary. This kind of documentary has the aura of a news report or investigative study. This documentary form is used commonly in television news specials and has its primary origins in the British films of the 30s and 40s produced by John Grierson, such as *Enough to Eat* and *Housing Problems*. The conventions of this form include interviews with people who either address the camera or an interviewer seen on camera. Authorities are presented who give infomation directly to the audience. There is heavy use made of supporting visual materials, such as maps, charts and graphs. Generally, such films present this data to lead to a clear social conclusion. In short, if one is to make a film to support the passage of a school bond bill, to elect a mayor, or to get people to donate money or to support a cause, then it should be a documentary of the social reconstruction type.

The third type of documentary is generally known as cinema verité or cinema truth. This is the process whereby one does indeed shoot an event as it is happening. This technique evolved over the past twenty years because equipment was developed which made it possible. This equipment includes lightweight portable cameras and sound equipment which can be carried, plus high speed film that can record a reasonable image, even in adverse lighting situations. It is really these technical changes which resulted in the conventions we call verité and recognize in the films of filmmakers like Don Pennebaker, Richard Leacock, Fred Wiseman and the Maysles brothers. The conventions for cinema verité include: (1) The use of the hand-held camera which often results in an unsteady, "newsreel" image. This type of image gives the impression that the action is taking place as we see it. (2) Use of the zoom (see the later section in this chapter on the use of the zoom for verité). (3) Location sound; that is, sound which is not always perfect and voices which are not always clearly audible. (4) A grainy, rough image, resulting from low light levels which require film with a greater speed.

The technique of cinema verité is quite useful in shooting an event or process which will have a beginning, middle and end—an event in which something will happen. Films about actors, teachers or coaches can be done verité. The problem with shooting verité is that a great deal of film is shot in order to capture enough of the event or process to make a worthwhile film.

The techniques of verité can be used to advantage to give the impression of things happening as we see them shot. Frequently, feature films will incorporate hand-held camera shots to give the impression of verité. *Dressed to Kill* and *Stardust Memories* have verité sequences which create an impression of spontaneity and immediacy. The British filmmaker Peter Watkins has done a number of films which are pseudo-verité, using all the techniques which would convince an audience that the action shown was shot as it happened, yet all of his films are staged. These include *The War Game, Culloden, Punishment Park* and *The Gladiators.*

Experimental. Documentary films rely on the viewer's belief that the presentation of reality, or its illusion, is important in itself. Many experimental films exist on the premise that the presentation of reality is insufficient, that art is based on the examination of a medium or on individual and personal creation. The more traditional experimental film, originating in various art movements in France and Germany in the 1920s, is that of the personal film. The premise is that films should be used for highly personal expression. Such films are a conscious statement of the personal life of the film artist as artist. The filmmaker or someone representing the filmmaker is the central figure, and the film depends on personal symbols. To understand the film, the viewer has to decode the filmmaker's symbols. Such films are frequently equated with the concept of lyric poetry and examples of this in feature films include the work of Jean Cocteau, Luis Bunuel, and Dennis Hopper.

It is important to recognize, however, that the making of a personal or symbolic film does not relieve the filmmaker of the need to understand the filmmaking process and what other personal filmmakers have done. Personal experimental films by young filmmakers tend to be, surprisingly, the least original of films. This is so because often the filmmaker does not realize that that which he considers personal and creative is often something that he shares with others and that his experiences are not at all unique. This leads to films frequently looking very much like other films of the genre. The filmmaker has much less access to personal films by others than he does to documentaries and narrative films. Therefore, he does not know what has already been done and has a tendency to go over old ground.

Thus, personal films frequently use metaphors of loneliness, people walking around in isolation, symbols of isolation including deserted beaches or parks, the sudden appearance of characters in bizarre dress, the disdain for a narrative line. Such films may intentionally break the rules of film narrative and violate principles of editing, screen direction, and camera technique. As discussed previously, it is important to know the rules before one can meaningfully break them. Picasso was, for example, a representational painter before he became interested in abstraction.

The second kind of experimental film is the formal film, the film in which the medium is used to examine itself. The formal experimental film is the quasi-equivalent of the abstract formal painting. Such experimental films draw attention to the fact that they are films, and experiment with time and space and the possibilities of film itself. Formal films exist which have single frame images, no images at all, repeated images and images drawn directly on the film. A film by Michael Snow called *Wavelength*, for example, consists of forty-five minutes of a single slow zoom across the room, emphasizing, among other things, the duration of time in a shot, the singularity of attention.

Narrative fiction. The vast majority of films seen and shot are story films. Generally, fictional story films accept the conventions of filmmaking. Such films, which include feature films and stories shot for television, are shared, not individual, experiences. These are films which depend on the idea of fiction as art or entertainment.

One can make popular genre films—westerns, gangster films, spy films, comedies—which are intended for entertainment or for an immediate escape from reality. They depend on different myths of heroes, groups of people, or villains, which the audience can recognize. The conventions vary for different genres, but such films basically accept the convention types that exist and recognize that a popular base is necessary if they are to succeed. These films accept that there are rules and expectations and work with the idea of meeting these expectations. The genre film is not necessarily limiting. Audiences know enough about westerns so that one need only establish a few visual ideas and character types—horses, costumes, certain kinds of behavior from character types—in order to create the setting for a western. When these are established, interesting themes, ideas or motifs can be investigated. For example, in a film like *The First Deadly Sin*, the audience knows from the start that the Frank Sinatra character is an archetype; he has appeared in hundreds of films and television series and novels. The directors, writers and actors can pass over detailed exposition and explanation of this character and his situation and delve directly into the details of the action and story. Furthermore, the archetype or the expectation of the archetype can be manipulated. The story and its development can create new dimensions for this character, dimensions which were not previously part of the archetype.

Another kind of narrative fiction film is the intellectual film. This type of film is often similar to the formal experimental film. Such films examine the formal aspects of film and art and politics and ideas. Within these films there is often frequent reference to and experimentation with filmic conventions and film genres. The films of Jean-Luc Godard, Jean Marie Straub and Michelangelo Antonioni are examples of the intellectual film.

The third kind of narrative film is the art film. These are like personal experimental films but usually are based on a broader, more universal set of codes and symbols than the personal film. Ingmar Bergman and Federico Fellini are perhaps the best known of contemporary art filmmakers. In their films, emotion and narrative line are basic, and techniques of genre film are accepted, but the ideas dealt with are not entertainment-oriented. These films deal with overt themes of love, God, death, responsibility, aging and dreams.

We do not believe that any one type of film is more important than any other. Documentaries, for example, are no more valuable to society or art than experimental films. The fact that experimental films may be personal does not automatically make them superior. In short, there should be no contest between the film supposedly reflecting reality and the film supposedly reflecting "pure" creation. It is simply a matter of which kind of film the filmmaker wants to make.

This is true, too, in relation to the narrative fiction film. A genre film (western, gangster, spy film) is no less meaningful or creative than an art film. All films are meaningful to audiences or audiences would not go to see them. A filmmaker need not analyze why the film is meaningful. It is enough that interest, curiosity, or pure entertainment can be created. To do any of these is perhaps the hardest thing in filmmaking. Therefore, it is entirely up to the filmmaker as to what kind of film or combinations of kinds he or she should make. The filmmaker should understand the filmmaking process and should know where his or her film stands in relation to the history and conventions of the various types of documentary, experimental and narrative fiction films.

Film Ideas

There are several writing stages which most films go through before actual production. These are: the original idea, the synopsis, the treatment, the action and dialogue script, the writer's shooting script and the director's shooting script or production script.

The original idea is exactly what its name implies. It is the original idea or conception for a film. The original idea is not a formal stage in pre-production; it usually exists in the writer's mind until such time as it is developed into a synopsis or treatment. However, it is good practice to write ideas down to preserve them, as they are easily forgotten.

It is often difficult to conceive of an idea for a film. There are several everyday sources for these ideas:

1.   One's own experience

2.   The experience of a friend or a story told by a friend

3.   A newspaper story

4.   An event or story on television or radio news

5.   A short story, novel, or play

6.   A song or poem

For a first filmmaking effort, it is usually advisable to choose ideas which involve action and movement. Complex ideas are more difficult to communicate in film, especially in short films. Therefore, for a first film, keep the ideas simple. Complex and abstract ideas can be experimented with as the potentials of the film medium are understood.

National news stories or "hot" news items are generally more difficult to deal with for several reasons. Usually the story is well known and therefore, the plot or story will be quite predictable from the start of the film. Also, the filmmaker's interpretation and translation of a current news event or story will be open to challenge and criticism. Therefore, in gathering ideas from newspaper, radio, or television, it is best to consider the smaller, human interest story as opposed to the headline story.

Many student films are based on an adaptation of a short story, novel, or play. Copyright is an important consideration in using someone else's work. It is against the law to make a film based on someone else's idea. In order to use an idea in film, the rights to that idea must be acquired. For student films, these legal considerations are often overlooked, as the films rarely go into commercial distribution. Therefore, adapting short stories, novels or plays is common practice for student and independent filmmakers. Consider the following when you adapt material:

1. Change the names of characters.

2. Change locations and settings.

3. Adapt the story from its literary format to a filmic format. Those elements of the story which have action and movement should be developed and expanded. Those aspects of the story which involve complex and abstract ideas and character's interior thoughts should be carefully thought about and translated into images which convey these ideas.

4. Avoid fictional ideas which depend heavily on a "payoff." There is always a temptation in short, narrative films to think of ideas that have a payoff ending, a twist or surprise at the end of the film. The danger here is that the main body of the film may tend to rely on the surprise ending. If the ending is anything less than brilliant, the film will be flawed, as essentially, the success of the film depends on the ending. If the idea being considered does have a payoff ending, it is important that the main body of the film be well developed and coherent, so that the film does not depend exclusively on the ending.

5. Consider ideas which do not make great demands on actors, unless very good actors are available. Acting for film is, to a great extent, looking natural, not performing. Therefore, film acting is often much more difficult than theatrical acting.

6. Avoid considering ideas which involve actors or resources that are unavailable. It is almost impossible to make a dingy apartment look like a mansion. It is equally difficult for a young man to portray an old man on film. A young man, dressed up and made up as an old man, may be convincing in the theater where the audience is at least 15 feet from the stage. But on film, where the audience comes face to face with the actor, it is much more difficult for the young man to be convincing as an old man.

Thus far, this discussion has centered on ideas for narrative fiction films. For documentary films, there are other factors which must be considered.

These apply especially to the short (5–10 minute) documentary film.

1. Choose a subject for a documentary which involves action and people doing things. The subject matter should be filmic. This is particularly true for non-lip sync documentaries. A film about a bank teller offers fewer visual and cinematic possibilities than a film about a local drag strip.

2. Think of ideas for documentary films which involve a process. In other words, think of making a documentary about a person or group of people involved in a process or event which has a beginning, middle and end. The process will provide a structure for the film. Thus, an idea for a film about a violin maker or a mime troupe rehearsing for a show is easier material to deal with in a short documentary film than an idea about a certain neighborhood or museum. The first two have built in structures, the completion of the finished violin and the evolution of a mime troupe show. The second two are more open ended and do not have a natural structure.

3. If a documentary idea is being considered which does not have an internal structure, then a structure can be created. This might be a simple structure, such as the beginning or ending of a day, or a framed structure, that is, a "bookending" device. Common framing devices are: opening and closing the film with the same shot or location, opening and closing the film with a voice-over, or opening and closing the film with a particular character doing a particular thing.

4. Permission to film in certain locations is often required. Therefore, do not seriously consider an idea for a documentary unless such permission can be secured. For example, do not develop an idea for a documentary film about a courtroom until permission to shoot the film has been granted.

5. Usually documentary films are more expensive films to make than fiction films. For most documentaries, a great deal more footage will be shot than is actually used in the final film. In most student and independent films, the cost of film stock processing is the major cost. For documentaries, twenty or thirty minutes of a process or event may be shot in order to make a 3–5 minute film.

Ideas and concepts for experimental films are more difficult to discuss, mainly because there are fewer guidelines for experimental films than for narrative and documentary films. It is quite difficult to define what an experimental film is. It is common to say that an experimental film is a type of film which is neither narrative nor documentary. But many experimental films have narrative and documentary elements. Perhaps the best definition of what constitutes an experimental film is to say that it foregrounds experiments with film conventions or ideas. Therefore, an experimental film examines, investigates, or theorizes about the technique and theory of film editing, narrative, visual style, character portrayal, or the perception of the film image on screen. By this definition, an experimental film could have either fictional or documentary components or both.

The preceding discussion has not been a thorough and comprehensive analysis of film ideas. Nor are the suggestions meant to be interpreted as hard and fast rules. Rather, the discussion is meant to serve as a guideline in the development of ideas for films of all types. A later chapter will discuss film ideas in detail. Ideas for each of the three modes of film just discussed might be:

A Narrative Fiction Idea. An idea for a film about a dart player who is a hustler. He hustles everyone he shoots against. He is the greatest dart player in the history of the game. Finally, in his biggest money game, his amazing skill fails him and he loses.

A Documentary Film Idea. A mime troupe is being formed in the theater department of a school. A film about the process whereby the troupe practices, rehearses and develops a mime show.

An Experimental Film Idea. A character goes to see a silent movie. At the movie theater, he walks into the screen and becomes involved in the action of the silent film.

The next pre-production step is the writing of the synopsis. A synopsis is the first prose description of a film idea. It should be a brief description of the action in the film. It should not include character description, dialogue or technical details. The synopsis is written so that the basic idea and action of the film can be communicated to prospective actors and technicians. This synopsis is actually a brief *treatment* for a film and for most student and independent films, the synopsis step is not necessary.

Film Treatments

The first formal step in pre-production is the preparation of the treatment. This is called a formal step because a treatment should always be

written for any type of film, whether it be a large budget Hollywood production like *Kramer vs. Kramer* or a five minute Super-8 film. In either
case, the treatment serves the following functions:

1. It can communicate in writing the main ideas, events and characters
   in the film to anyone who reads it.

2. It will help the filmmaker foresee any problems in securing locations and actors.

3. It will help in the organization of the sequence of events in the
   film, so that writing the script is made easier.

The form of the treatment is quite simple. It is a chronological, prose
description of all the action in the film. It should include: the title or
working title of the film, the gauge of the film and whether the film will
be in black and white or color, all scenes, all action and events, all locations, all characters with character descriptions, the type of sound to be
used in the film (whether it will be sync or music or presence), the intent
or purpose for making the film, and any problems that can be foreseen in
the making of the film and how these problems will be overcome.

The treatment should not include dialogue or word-by-word description
of voice-over or narration, except where the dialogue or voice-over is
essential to the understanding of the film. Similarly, it should not include
special effects, except where they are essential to the understanding of
the film.

The treatment should be concise and to the point. It should be clear and
easily readable. Imagery belongs in the film, not in the treatment. A treatment for most feature films is between 40 and 60 pages long. The treatment for most short films (3–5 minutes) need not be longer than ½ to ¾
of a page. The following are three treatments from the germ ideas discussed earlier:

1. Narrative Fiction Film Treatment.

*The main character, Bob, is a listless young man in
his 20s. He goes to a bar and is invited by a friend to
play a game of darts. He has never played before. He
loses the game but enjoys playing. He goes to a
store and buys a dart board and some darts. He practices at home a great deal. He becomes very involved
in the game. He gets better and better. Finally, he
becomes so good that he can throw a dart to any
spot on the board at will. He goes back to the bar*

and plays again. He hustles his friend and wins. His friend introduces him to another dart player—the best player at the bar. Bob plays again and wins. Bob is home practicing again. He discovers that he can throw the darts perfectly, even with his eyes closed. He can throw them perfectly with his back to the dart board. The darts seem to have a magical quality. He goes to another bar and beats everyone. Tex, the best dart thrower in the city, comes into the bar. He challenges Bob. They agree to play for a large sum of money. They start to play. Bob decides it's time to stop hustling. He starts to show off—throwing with his eyes closed, throwing with his back to the dart board, etc. Everyone is amazed. Suddenly, Bob starts to lose his touch. He can no longer throw perfectly. Tex starts to catch up in the game. Bob stops fooling around and tries very hard. But the magic touch is gone. Tex pulls ahead and wins. Bob leaves the bar dejectedly.

In the final scene, we see Bob going to play pool with a friend. He has never played before. He plays and loses but enjoys the game. He goes to a store to buy a pool cue.

Tentative title: *The Liveliest Dart*
Estimated length: 15 minutes
Possible production problems: shooting in bars, viewers following dart game

2. **Documentary Film Treatment.**
A mime troupe is being formed at the university and will be under the direction of a faculty member. Initial auditions begin in early March and rehearsals will continue through the end of May. At that time, the troupe will present a show to the public, entitled An Evening of Mime. None of the fifteen members in the troupe have had any prior experience in the art of mime. The film will attempt to capture the evolving process whereby a group of individuals learn the art of mime and come together as an interacting mime troupe. The filming will be sync sound,

hand held verité style. All rehearsal and exercise sessions will be attended by the camera crew.

The anticipated problems are that the presence of the camera crew and the filmmaking process will interfere with the process of the formation of the troupe. Hopefully, the camera crew will become involved in the process and will be considered a part of the process.

There is always the possibility that the process will not be as visible as is hoped. Or a conflict might develop among the troupe or between the troupe and the faculty supervisor. If for some reason, this small group process is less successful and cinematic than anticipated, the film will evolve into an educational film on the training and practice of the art of mime.

Tentative titles: *Mime Troupe, Any Empty Space*
Primary shooting location: Speech Building
    Auditorium
Estimated length: 30–40 minutes
Estimated budget: $6,000

3. Treatment for Narrative Film With Experimental Elements.

A moustached, shabbily dressed young man goes to a local theater where silent films are shown. He sees photographs of the players in the film outside the theater. We see that he thinks the leading lady of the silent film is very beautiful. He goes into the theater, past the theater owner who remarks to himself that the theater is getting a less respectable audience than it did in the past. The young man buys some popcorn and candy from the candy counter girl, who is busy watching television. The young man enters the theater, and as he goes down the aisle, has his popcorn box knocked out of his hand by a child running up the aisle.

Before the film begins, the theater manager comes on stage and announces that this is the last showing of silent films in the theater. The theater is going to switch to adult films. He also announces that for the last showing, a pianist will play. The pianist takes a bow and the film begins.

We see the silent film, a melodrama about a girl—

the girl the young man had admired in the photo-graph—and her mother who are victims of the villain who plans to marry the girl. To this point, the film is not experimental. However, the young man is upset by the helplessness of the girl in the film and gets up to help her. In spite of cries from the audience, the young man climbs up on the stage and plunges into the silent film. The villain grabs him and throws him out of the screen and back onto the stage. The relationship of film and audience is foregrounded experimentally, but in a narrative context. Since the silent film is black and white and silent, it also presents a conventional contrast with the rest of the film.

The determined young man gets up and plunges back into the picture again. From then on, we see the young man in a variety of misadventures as he is carried from shot to shot in the silent film. In each shot, he remains the same size and in the same position as the previous shot, thus foregrounding the convention of the cut covering a jump in time and space. At first, he plunges into a wedding cake and falls into a pool because he does not know where he will be from shot to shot, since the silent film keeps moving on. Finally, after a wild ride on top of a car bringing the best man with the ring for the wedding, the young man learns how to control his constant movement from shot to shot. He grabs the wedding ring, traps the villain in a window and marries the girl. All of this action is intercut with shots of the theater audience reacting and the piano player playing.

Just before the wedding takes place in the silent film, the young man writes a note and turns it to the audience. It invites the people in the theater to come to the wedding. We then see the ticket taker, candy counter girl and members of the audience climb on the stage and enter the silent movie. The wedding continues and the end credit comes on as the camera pulls back to reveal the screen and the piano player, now playing in an empty theater.

Tentative title: *Last Minute Marriage*
Estimated length: 15 minutes

Film Scripts

The next formal pre-production stage, after the preparation of the treatment, is the writing of the film script. As mentioned previously, there are several forms of the film script. These are the action and dialogue script, the writer's shooting script, and the director's shooting script or production script. All these forms represent variations on a shot by shot or scene by scene breakdown of the action of the film.

The action and dialogue script is a script form rendering of the locations, action, and dialogue by characters in the film. The script is broken down into scenes, but not necessarily into separate shots. Few technical details, such as camera placement or movement or special effects, such as fades or dissolves, are included. The main function of the action and dialogue script is to provide a rough scene by scene or location by location breakdown of the main action of the film. An action and dialogue script is usually not necessary for short, non-lip sync films.

The preparation of the writer's shooting script is the next formal pre-production step. The writer's shooting script is a very elaborate delineation of all shots, locations, characters, action, sound, and technical details of the film. This type of script serves a variety of functions:

1. The script is a breakdown of all shots. This eliminates the possibility of forgetting a particular shot.

2. It divides the film into separate locations. Therefore, all locations can be scouted and the possible shooting problems inherent in these locations can be foreseen. Also, the location breakdown will help in determining the appropriate film stock for that location.

3. The script includes all camera placements and movements and all special effects. Therefore, the writer's shooting script is essential in the planning and execution of difficult shots, special effects, etc.

4. The script can be a guide in determining the exact length of the film. By mentally timing out the length of each shot, the overall length of the film can be fairly accurately gauged. This can be especially useful in determining how much film stock will be needed and therefore, what the total budget of the film will be.

5. The script provides a breakdown for the actors as to which shots and scenes they will appear in and therefore, when they will be needed during shooting.

6. As will be discussed later in this chapter, the writer's shooting script provides a reference for the breakdown of shots and scenes into a shooting order.

There are a variety of terms which are usually used to describe shots in a writer's shooting script. These terms and their abbreviations are:

EXTREME LONG SHOT (ELS)—	Used to depict vast areas and to orient the viewer. Also known as *ESTABLISHING LONG SHOT.*
LONG SHOT (LS)—	Used to depict the entire area of the action.
MEDIUM LONG SHOT (MLS)—	Used to depict a full length view of an actor or of the action, but not of the full set.
MEDIUM SHOT (MS)—	Used to depict an actor above the knees or below the waist to the head. It may involve several actors as stated (a *TWO SHOT* or *THREE SHOT*), but it is able to reveal facial expressions.
MEDIUM CLOSE-UP (MCU)—	Used to depict an actor midway between the waist and shoulders to above the head.
CLOSE-UP (CU)—	Used to depict an actor from just below the shoulders to above the head.
EXTREME CLOSE-UP (ECU)—	Used to depict the actor's head or some closer portion of the actor's face or body.
OVER THE SHOULDER SHOT (OSS)—	Used to depict the back of the neck and shoulder of one actor on one side of the screen while another actor is open to the camera.
PAN—	When the camera moves on its horizontal axis.
TILT—	When the camera moves on its vertical axis.
DOLLY SHOT—	When the camera moves into or away from a subject. Shot should be described as *DOLLY IN* or *DOLLY OUT.*
TRACKING SHOT—	When the camera moves on tracks with a moving subject.

BOOM SHOT—	When the camera moves upwards or downwards. The shot should be described as *BOOM UP* or *BOOM DOWN.*
LOW ANGLE SHOT—	When the camera is placed below eye level and tilted upwards.
HIGH ANGLE SHOT—	When the camera is placed above eye level and tilted downwards.
REACTION SHOT—	Used to depict an actor listening and reacting to another actor's dialogue or movement.
ZOOM—	Used to bring the image from wide angle to telephoto by narrowing the angle of view of the lens (*ZOOM IN*) or to bring the image from telephoto to wide angle (*ZOOM OUT*) by enlarging the angle of view.
FADE —	Used when the shot is to gradually disappear into black (*FADE OUT*) or to gradually appear out of black *(FADE IN)*.
DISSOLVE —	The overlapping of the fading out of one shot with the fading in of another, giving the impression that the second shot appears out of the first. Also sometimes called LAP DISSOLVE.
WIPE —	Two shots in which the second pushes the first off the screen (optical effect).
FREEZE FRAME —	Freezing the action of a shot by repeated printing of a single frame (optical effect).
SUPERIMPOSITION —	Overlapping two or more images so that these two or more images can be seen on the screen at the same time.

The seven shot descriptions used to indicate the camera's position in regard to the action or subject (ELS, LS, MLS, MS, MCU, CU and ECU) are relative to the action or subject. Generally, they are used to describe the framing for a person in the shot. If these shot descriptions are used to describe actions or subjects which do not include people, then they must be considered relative to the action or subject in the shot.

The form of the writer's shooting script is quite important. If the form is consistent, actors and technicians will find the script easy to follow. Here is an example of the proper script form for the writer's shooting script:

Writer's Shooting Script

```
FADE IN

EXT. ENTRANCE MERIWETHER HOSPITAL -- DAY

1. LS MEADES ENTER CAB

    A parked cab is waiting outside the Meriwether hospital. MR.
    and MRS. MEADE, a typically American young couple, come out
    and enter the cab. They are followed out by a NURSE holding
    a baby. She waits outside the cab to hand them the baby.


2. MS NURSE HANDS BABY

    The NURSE hands the bundled baby to its mother and father
    in the cab.

                            NURSE
                    There you are, Mrs. Meade.


    INT. CAB -- DAY

3. MS MEADES RECEIVE BABY

    From inside the cab, shooting past MR. and MRS. MEADE, we
    see the NURSE outside the car as she hands the baby to
    its father and mother.

                        MRS. MEADE
                        (fearfully)
                Will the ride hurt him, nurse?

                            NURSE
                        (smiling)
                He'll live through it, I'm sure.

                        MR. MEADE
                        (hesitantly)
                I can hold him, dear.
```

> MRS. MEADE
> Oh! He's not heavy at all, darling.

EXT. CAB AT CURB -- DAY

4. MS NURSE BIDS FAREWELL

We see the NURSE as MR. MEADE'S hand slips a bill into her
hand.

> MR. MEADE
> (off screen)
> Thanks for everything, nurse.

The NURSE slams the cab door shut and grins.

> NURSE
> Thank you!

The NURSE straightens up.

> NURSE
> (continues)
> ...He's all yours now. Watch
> out for kidnappers! 'Bye!

5. LS CAR PULLS AWAY -- NURSE GOES IN -- CRASH

From a HIGH ANGLE we see the car pull out of frame. The camera
BOOMS DOWN and DOLLIES IN to a CU of the NURSE as she stares
after it for a moment, sighs, shrugs her shoulders, turns to
the hospital entrance and walks toward it as the CAMERA PANS
with her. As she passes the sign on the wall reading "Meri-
wether Hospital," the CAMERA HOLDS and lets her exit frame.
The CAMERA DOLLIES IN for an ECU of the sign. Shortly after
the CAMERA has stopped on the sign, we hear in the distance
the SOUND of a car CRASHING violently.

DISSOLVE

The writer's shooting script for a verité documentary is often difficult
to prepare. Usually a documentary such as this is "scripted" in the editing

room. That is, the script or shot-by-shot breakdown for the film is created on the basis of the footage filmed. Therefore, a pre-production shot by shot delineation of the action is impossible. What should be included in the writer's shooting script for a verité documentary is the following:

1. All logistical and technical details that pertain to the filming of the documentary.

2. A list of many possible shots and camera set-ups. These need not be in the order they will appear in the film.

3. A discussion of the structure of the film. Here, ideas for possible linear and framed structures for the film should be mentioned.

The director's shooting script, or actual production script, is usually an elaboration of the writer's shooting script. The production script is based on a thorough scouting of all locations, the choice of actors who will play the various roles in the film, and the equipment to be used for the shooting of the film. The writer's shooting script can be developed into a production script through the use of notes and diagrams. The notes should contain exact information as to the execution of each shot and should include character placement, movement and gesture, as well as camera placement or movement. The diagrams can be bird's-eye views of character and camera positions.

It is usually not necessary to prepare a production script for a documentary. The details in the writer's shooting script are sufficient to start actual production.

Script Breakdown and Pre-Production Planning

A shooting order for the shots in the film can be compiled from the production script. Because of the difficulties in camera set-ups and lighting it is not always desirable and efficient to shoot the film in the order indicated by the script. Instead, the script is broken down into a shooting order based on camera position. There are two basic approaches to the breakdown and shooting order for shots and scenes in the film. These are the *master scene technique* and the *triple take technique.*

The master scene technique is the approach most often used in shooting full length, narrative films. A scene is shot in its entirety in an MS or MLS. Then the entire scene or parts of the scene are re-shot from different camera angles. These may be close-ups of various characters in the scene, extreme close-ups, and two-shots (two people). The various shots are then cut together in the editing room according to the script. The master scene approach affords the actors the opportunity of acting out and therefore, understanding the scene in its entirety, rather than having to act out or develop the scene in short shots from different angles. This approach also makes for greater flexibility in the editing room. With the master scene technique, there is usually a wide variety of shots and camera angles to choose from. Thus, problems in match cutting and editing tempo and pacing can be overcome more easily. The main disadvantage to the master scene technique is that the shooting ratio is greatly increased and if employed for a student film, the budget, necessarily, becomes much higher.

The triple take technique is an approach which adheres more closely to the actual shots as scripted. It is a more efficient approach in terms of actual footage shot. In using the triple take technique, there are *three* things to think of:

1. The shot in the script being filmed.

2. The shot in the script that came before the one being filmed.

3. The shot in the script that follows the one being filmed.

Thus while shooting any shot, the filmmaker should be thinking in terms of the preceding and following script shots in terms of matching action, camera angle, and screen direction. Usually this means shooting with a certain overlap from shot to shot to make editing easier. But in this case, it means that for shooting a particular shot, the shots in the script coming before and after the one being filmed must be considered. The advantage of this technique is that by shooting each shot as scripted, the shooting ratio, and therefore the budget, will be lower. There are several disadvantages to this triple take technique. First, it is more difficult for the actors to understand and execute a particular scene when it is broken up into disjointed bits and pieces. Second, because the film is shot only from those camera placements called for in the script, greater editing problems can be anticipated.

It is possible to combine the master scene and triple take techniques in planning the shooting of a film. Therefore, for complex scenes, shoot a master scene of the entire scene and then shoot selected close-ups and two-shots as called for in the script. It is generally good practice to record master shots from a fixed camera position. While shooting the master shot, avoid using pans, tilts or zooms. This will make cutting back and forth from the master shot easier and smoother. For simple scenes, plan to use the triple take technique to conserve film stock.

A shooting schedule example from a production script follows:

Production: <u>Last Minute Marriage</u>

Dates: June 10-20 (dates subject to change according
       to weather)

Monday 10th	shot #s	crew	cast
AM & PM	2-10	animator & assistant	none

Tues. 11th

| AM ext theater | 1,13,12 | full shooting crew | Malcolm, ticket girl |
| PM int theater | 14,17,16,15, 18,20,22,19, 21,24 | "   "   " | "   " , manager, candy woman, audience |

Weds. 12th

| AM int theater | 25,26-28,27, 30,32-35(reactions), 35,37,38,39 | "   "   " | Malcolm, manager, audience |

Fri. 14th

| AM int living rm | (40-51), 42, 44 46,48,41,47,45 | "   " | Margaret, mother Pierre, Malcolm |
| PM "   "   " | 49,50,51,65,66 | | |

Sat. 15th

| AM ext pool | 58 | "   "   " | Malcom, women, Pierre, Margaret, |
| PM ext lawn | (52-56), 55, 52, 54, 56, 53 | "   "   " | mother, guests, theater, audience |

Sun. 16th

| AM int kitchen | 57,(59-62), 62 59,61,60,63,64 | silent shooting crew only | Malcolm, Pierre, Margaret |
| PM "   " | | | |

( ) indicates master scene

17th, 18th, 19th and 20th to be kept open for <u>reshooting</u>

In addition to the shooting schedule, it is advisable for complex scenes to prepare a complete prop and equipment list and a crew list. For example:

date	props	equipment
Mon. 10th	still photos only	animation
Tues. 11th		
AM	poster, tickets, Keaton poster	ext. shooting pack
PM	tickets, popcorn, T.V.	int. shooting pack (special lights)
Weds. 12th	same as above	same as above
Fri. 14th		
AM	cigars, newspaper, hat	int. shooting pack
PM	photo of Margaret	" " "
Sat. 15th		
AM	raft	ext. shooting pack
PM	chairs, ring, pens, rug	" " "
Sun. 16th		
AM	cake, table, knife	silent int. pack
PM	" " "	" " "

<u>Interior shooting pack</u>

camera and accessories
recorder and accessories
4 1000W lights
4 light stands
6 ext. cords
tripod

<u>Ext. shooting pack</u>

camera and accessories
recorder and accessories
tripod

Full shooting crew	Silent shooting crew	Animation crew
camera – Lou	camera – Lou	animator – Don
asst. camera – Dave	asst. camera – Dave	assistant – Jean
director – Stu	director – Stu	director – Stu
sound – Larry	lighting – Mary	
asst. sound – Bill	asst. lighting – John	
lighting – Mary		
asst. lighting – John		
continuity – Ed		

All these pre-production steps are taken for one primary reason, to make the shooting of the film go as smoothly and efficiently as possible. These preparations are particularly important in dealing with volunteer actors and crew. The actual shooting of a film is usually a long and laborious process. When the filmmaker is prepared for a shooting session, the actors and crew will know what to do and when. Therefore, they will be more committed to the project.

Of course, the amount of pre-production planning is dependent to a large extent on the complexity of the film. Considerably less preparation than outlined here is necessary for short films involving only one actor and a few locations. In the production of feature films, there is often a great difference in the degree of pre-production planning. This difference is often a matter of the methods of a particular director. Alfred Hitchcock, for example, was noted for his meticulous preparation in the shooting of his films. Every scene and shot was elaborately planned and rehearsed before it was shot. Very little was left to chance. Conversely, the French director Jean-Luc Godard prefers to work very loosely and spontaneously. Often in a Godard film, the actual dialogue and camera movement for a particular shot will not be determined until the camera is actually recording the shot. The advantage to this approach is that it creates the possibility for interesting results based on chance and spontaneity. The disadvantage is that a great deal of film and time can be wasted in trying to come up spontaneously with good results. Thoughtful pre-production planning is important in first filmmaking efforts. There are a multitude of immediate logistical problems in the shooting of any film. These include lighting, exact camera placement and movement, and actor positioning and blocking. It is very difficult to make decisions regarding all these factors on the shooting set and still keep a clear idea of what the film is to be about. A well-planned shooting session will often enhance the possibility of interesting spontaneous results.

③ Production

When pre-production planning is complete, it is time to move on to the production or actual shooting stage of the film. The production stage will be the subject of this chapter.

Camera Placement

The first and most obvious consideration on location or in a studio is where to place the camera in relation to the action to be filmed. The determination of camera placement is extremely important and should be made after careful deliberation. There are always logistical reasons for one camera placement over another. For example, if a shot takes place in a small room and the script calls for a long shot or medium long shot, it may be necessary to move the camera out of the room and shoot through a doorway to achieve the desired framing and thereby record all the action. Or in another room, the furniture may have to be rearranged so that there is room for the camera and actors. But these are basically practical and logistical aspects of camera placement, and are dealt with relative to the action called for in the shot and on the location.

A more fundamental consideration in camera placement is the camera's relationship to the action and the implications inherent in this relationship. A simpler way of discussing this is to speak of the camera's involvement in the action. It must always be remembered that the camera is a recording device. The way it is used as a recording device, its relationship to the action it is recording, and its involvement in that action are very important. There are three basic types of shots that convey three different ways that the camera is involved in the action. These are the *objective shot,* the *subjective shot,* and the *point of view shot.*

In the **objective shot**, the camera records the action as if the action were being seen by an unseen, impartial observer (Fig. 3-1). This is the most non-involving type of shot. It is also the most common type of shot used in filmmaking. It is, as its name states, objective; the camera is used only to record the action and is not involved in it. Objective shots are usually long shots and medium shots, although they sometimes can be used for close-ups.

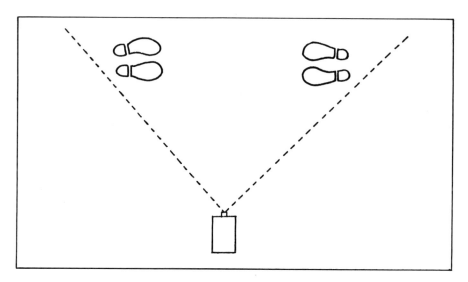

Fig. 3-1. The objective shot.

A **subjective shot** is one in which the camera records the shot as if it were being seen through the eyes of a character (Fig. 3-2). Thus, in a subjective shot, the camera must "behave" as the character it represents behaves. For example, consider a scene in which a character is running through the woods. To create a subjective shot in this scene, the camera-person must literally turn on the camera and run through the woods with it. The subjective shot is the most involving type of shot. It involves the audience directly with the action and with the character who is part of that action. In the 1920s, German filmmakers experimented extensively with this type of shot. In German silent films of the 20s, if a character swings on a trapeze, as in *Variety*, the action will be recorded in a subjective shot. The camera, representing the character swinging, will twist and turn and roll. Similarly, in German silents, if a character is drunk, as in *Uberfall*, then in the subjective shot the camera will record a blurry image or it might stagger or appear dizzy.

Although the subjective shot is the most involving type of shot, it is also the most difficult type of shot to use in a film. Because it literally represents the visual perceptions of a character, it presents certain basic problems. First, when using a subjective shot, conventional editing techniques are usually abandoned. When the camera sees what a character sees, it is inconsistent to edit or cut to a different shot of what the same character is seeing because human perceptions do not "edit." Therefore, when using a subjective shot, it is conventional to cut to an objective one which shows the character whose perceptions were seen in the subjective shot.

Objective shot.

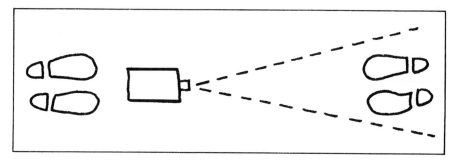

Fig. 3-2. The subjective shot.

Another problem encountered when using subjective shots is that when the camera represents the eyes of a character, other characters must look directly into the lens if they are to relate to that character. When this happens in the projected film, those characters looking into the lens seem to be looking directly at the audience. This will tend to break down the illusion of reality in a narrative film. It does this by making the audience suddenly aware of the process that went into making the film while they are viewing it.

The existence of these two factors involving the use of subjective shots does not preclude their use in all types of films. In general, subjective shots will work best in an action situation, where it is desirable to deeply involve the audience. An example of this is in a chase scene through the woods where the police are pursuing an escaped convict:

```
EXT. DAY

1. MS ESCAPED CONVICT RUNNING THROUGH THE WOODS

   The CONVICT is out of breath, running through the woods. CAMERA
   PANS left to right to follow him. He pauses and looks over his
   shoulder for his pursuers.

2. MS POLICE IN WOODS, IN PURSUIT

   The two policemen, with guns drawn, are chasing the CONVICT.
   CAMERA PANS with them.

3. CU CONVICT

   He is sweating as he is running. He enters the thick brush of
   the woods.

4. MS SUBJECTIVE SHOT, THROUGH CONVICT'S EYES
   With HAND HELD CAMERA, the woods stream by.
```

Subjective shot. The character looks directly into the lens.

5. MS CONVICT RUNNING IN WOODS

He is getting more tired and his pace is slowing. Again, he
pauses to look back at his pursuers.

In this example, the subjective shot (shot no. 4) involves the audience directly in the action. The problem of editing is avoided because shot number 4 is "bookended" by objective shots of the convict. The problem of other characters looking into the lens is avoided because, in the subjective shot, the convict does not encounter anyone.

The **point of view shot** is a type of shot which, in its relationship to the action, falls somewhere between an objective and a subjective shot (Fig. 3-3). That is to say, point of view shots are more involving than objective shots and less involving than subjective shots. In terms of camera position, the point of view (or POV) camera is placed midway between a subjective and an objective placement.

The POV shot is usually used when there are two or more characters in a scene. A POV shot is near to, but not directly from, a character's point of view. It is usually a close-up. A character included in a POV shot does not look into the lens, but rather looks to the left or right of the lens. A POV shot is more involving than an objective shot because the camera is more directly involved in the action. The great advantage of a POV shot is that it has none of the problems of the subjective shot. There are no

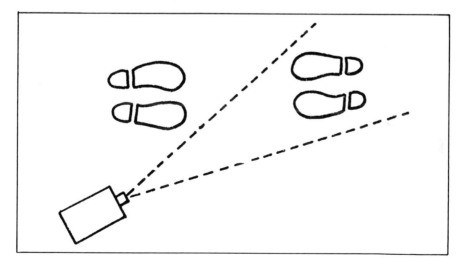

Fig. 3-3. A point-of-view shot.

Point-of-view shot. In this instance, it is an "over-the-shoulder" POV.

problems with editing and there is never the problem of characters looking into the lens. The exact placement of the camera for a POV shot is
determined by the position of the character from whose point of view
(approximately) the shot will be taken. This means that the camera should
be at the same height and to the side of that character.

POV shots are most often used to involve the audience in the inter-
action between two characters. However, in certain instances, a POV shot
can be used when the shot involves only one character. When used in this
way, the POV shot represents what the character "sees." Going back to the
example of the escaped convict in the woods:

```
     EXT. DAY

  1. MS CONVICT RUNNING THROUGH WOODS

     Convict is out of breath, running through the woods.

  2. CU CONVICT RUNNING THROUGH WOODS

     He pauses and looks back at his pursuers.

  3. MS CONVICT'S POV, THE POLICE IN THE DISTANCE

     The police are pursuing the convict.

  4. MS CONVICT TURNS AND STARTS RUNNING AGAIN

     He turns quickly and begins running faster. He exits frame
     right.
```

Here, shot no. 3 is a POV to represent what the convict sees as he turns
and looks back. This is not a subjective shot because the camera does not
behave as a character, the convict. It is tripod mounted and steady. As
with the POV shots discussed earlier, the camera placement for this type
of character "seeing" POV is actually to the side of the character. Therefore, if the police were to look at the convict in shot no. 3, they would
look to the side of the lens, not into it. This type of character "seeing"
POV is usually preceded by an objective close-up. This is so that the audience will know from whose point of view the shot is being taken. Sometimes the POV shot can come first and be followed by an objective close-
up (Fig. 3-4).

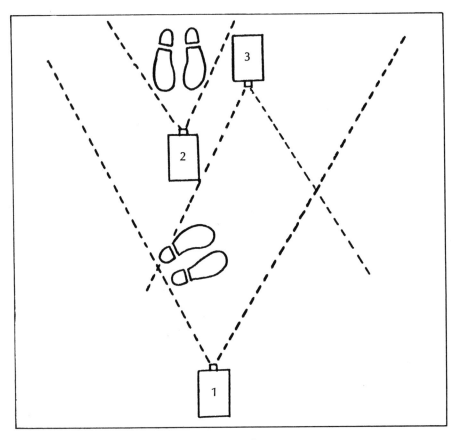

Fig. 3-4. A character point-of-view "seeing" shot.

Camera Angles

With the fundamentals of the camera's relationship to the action in mind, the next consideration is the specifics of camera placement or camera angles. A discussion of camera angles involves two factors, the vertical and horizontal planes of the camera in relation to the shot.

The vertical plane, or camera height, encompasses five types of placement (Fig. 3-5).

The various types of vertical placements have been assumed to have psychological implications for the subject being shot and have led to conventions of use. These conventional implications are:

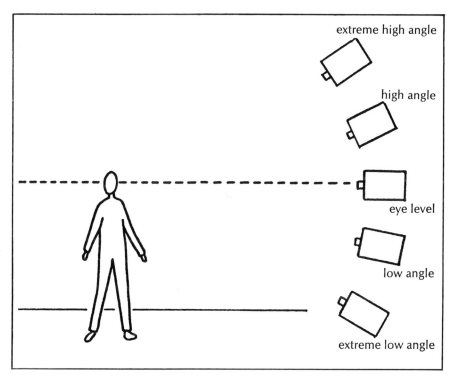

Fig. 3-5. Five vertical camera placements.

1. Eye level angles are neutral and inherently imply nothing specific.

2. Higher than eye level angles (high angle and extreme angle) suggest that the subject being filmed is weak, dominated by forces around him or her, and/or is not in control of the situation.

3. Lower than eye level angles (low angle and extreme low angle) suggest that the subject being filmed is strong, dominant, and in control of the situation around him or her.

The reasons for these conventions may, perhaps, be simple. An eye level camera angle is neutral because the audience viewing the shot from this angle will be on an equal level with the subject or action being filmed. In viewing a shot taken from a higher than eye level angle, the audience is looking down on the subject or action and, therefore, that subject or action will seem smaller, weaker, and by implication, dominated. The opposite holds true for shots taken from a low angle. Remember, these are conventions that have developed through the history of film and not

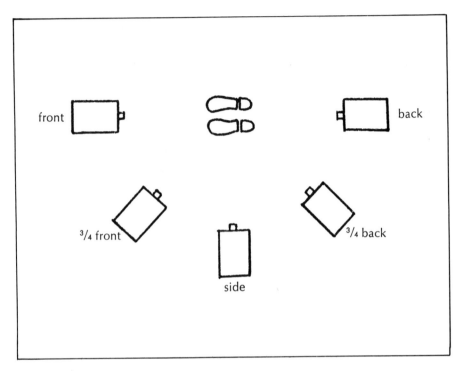

Fig. 3-6. Five horizontal camera placements.

necessarily unchangeable truths. If you decide not to go along with such conventions, you should be aware of what you are doing and the fact that your audience might misunderstand.

The horizontal plane of the camera also encompasses five types of placements (Fig. 3-6).

The various types of horizontal camera placements also have conventions for the subject or action being filmed. These conventions are most evident when the shot is a close-up of a person. Bear in mind that these are not rules. The exceptions are easy to find. They are, however, conventional assumptions that will help you until you feel confident enough to experiment on your own.

1. A back angle for a person is the weakest. The audience cannot see his or her face.

2. Three-quarter back is the second weakest. The action still cannot be seen.

3. The profile angle is considerably stronger than either back or ¾ back, because the audience can see at least half of the person's face.

4. The ¾ front shot is the strongest shot of that person. The fact that the person is at a ¾ angle toward the lens makes his or her character strong. The angling gives the frame depth and by extension, the character has depth.

5. The full front angle is quite strong, but actually is not as strong as the ¾ front. In the full front, the face has only two dimensions as opposed to the ¾ front, in which the face has three.

The choice of camera angle is in many cases dependent upon the type of shot—either objective, subjective, or POV—which is being used. As discussed earlier, if the shot is a POV or a subjective shot, then the camera angle is already established. For a subjective shot, the camera is placed exactly in the position of the character whose perception it represents. For a POV shot, the camera is placed at the same height and to the side of the character whose point of view is represented by the shot (Fig. 3-7). In using these two types of shots, then, the implications of camera angle will devolve out of the character placement and relationships within the scene. For example:

A is higher than B in the frame. Consequently, A's point of view shot of B will be from a high angle and a point of view shot of A will be from a low angle. It should then be clear that to exploit the psychological implications while using POV shots, actors can be placed in certain relationships so that the POV shots will convey these implications. In the example above, the POV shots will reinforce A's dominance over B.

The convention for camera angles in objective shots is—usually shoot at eye level and from a horizontal angle which will best capture all the action. This is most often a "side line" view point. The reasons for this are clear. This camera placement offers the most comprehensive view of the action. Therefore, at eye level (5–6 feet above the ground), the audience will have the best perception of the action. The side line vantage point, as opposed to a vantage point behind one character or another, also gives a good perspective of the action. There are exceptions to this principle:

1. Often a long shot or an extreme long shot is best shot from a high angle. This provides a better vantage point for the action.

2. Occasionally, it is advisable to shoot a master objective shot, medium shot, or medium long shot, at a higher than eye level angle if there is relevant foreground action. The higher angle will make

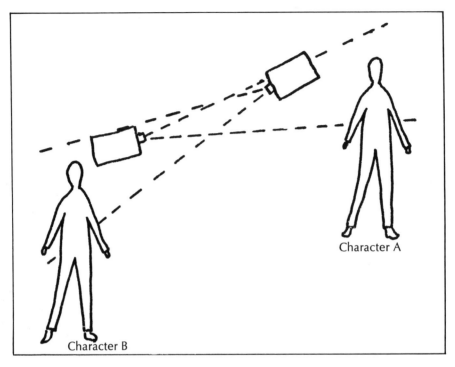

Fig. 3-7. POV camera angles resulting from character placement within a scene.

foreground action easier to see. An example of this is found in Don Siegel's *Baby Face Nelson*. In one scene, where Baby Face Nelson has had his fingerprints changed and is at a desk checking them, the master objective shot is at a slightly higher than eye level angle. This makes it easier to see Nelson checking his fingerprints.

3. Shooting at slightly lower than eye level will make movement seem faster. It is, therefore, sometimes desirable to shoot objective shots of things moving from low angles to make them seem to be going faster.

Composition

The composition of an image is one of the more difficult aspects of cinematography to discuss. It is usually inappropriate to speak in terms of good and bad composition. One should, instead, consider the effectiveness or lack of effectiveness of a particular composition in relation to the action, motion, and content of a particular shot. Although effective com-

positions are, for the most part, a matter or personal judgment and preference, there are several guidelines to achieving effective composition
which we would offer:

The Principle of Thirds. This is a general principle for composing an
image which is based on the horizontal and vertical division of the frame
by lines or masses or forms. Essentially, the principle of thirds means that
more effective compositions are usually achieved by dividing the frame by
thirds, rather than by bisecting the frame. Thus in composing for horizontals, such as the horizon, it is often preferable to place the horizon at
the top third or the bottom third of the frame, rather than at the middle of
the frame.

The first composition, with the horizon in the bottom third of the frame,
lends a feeling of openness and freedom to the image. When the horizon
is placed along the top third of the frame, the image may indicate a much
more confined and restricted environment.

The principle of thirds applies to the verticals in the frame as well. Thus,
a close-up of a person looking at something is usually framed as follows:

Here, the person's head is in the left-hand third of the frame and the
right-hand two thirds of the frame provide a looking area for the person.
If this image is framed with the person in the center of the frame, the
composition might be considered unbalanced.

The principle of thirds also applies when panning with a moving object.
Here the object is led by two thirds of the frame to allow a freedom of
movement and create balance.

Depth in the Image. Effective compositions are often the result of achieving a sense of depth in the two dimensional film image. This illusion of
depth can be created in several ways. Diagonals within the frame often
lend depth to an image. Objects filmed at oblique angles rather than
head-on will result in diagonals and will, therefore, create depth. A framing device within the frame will create depth. Thus, a door frame or a
window on an outer edge of the film frame will add depth to the shot.

Foreground and background objects in the frame also create depth.
Similarly, two or more levels of action within the frame give the image
depth.

Horizontals and Verticals Along the Edge of the Frame. When horizontal
or vertical lines or forms or masses are included along the edge of the
frame, they are usually clearly in frame. A vertical that is just barely touching one edge of the frame can be visually displeasing. Also, when using
vertical or horizontal lines close to frame lines, it is usually more effective
to make the lines run exactly parallel to the frame line. If the horizontals

The horizon bisects the frame.

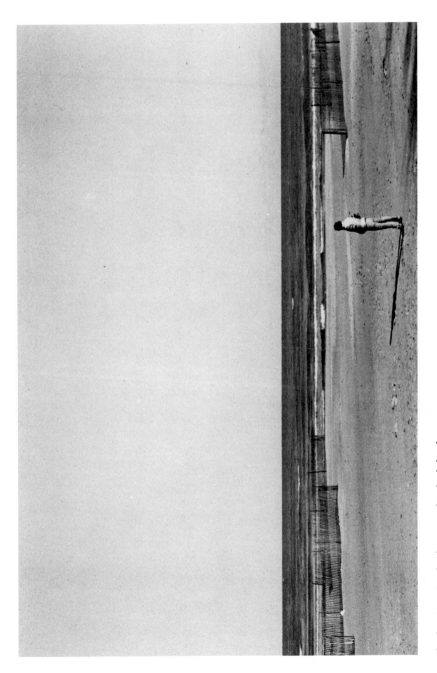

The horizon in the bottom third of the frame.

The horizon in the top third of the frame.

The framing provides a "looking" area for the actor.

The actor is centered in the frame and no "looking" area is provided.

A framing device to create depth in the image.

Foreground and background objects in the frame to create depth.

Another example of depth in the image.

or verticals are not parallel with the frame line, the frame can appear out of balance.

Experience in working with visual images helps to develop a sense of what constitutes an effective composition. Therefore, one's personal preference should serve as the ultimate guideline.

Screen Direction and Continuity

A very important element in filmmaking is the principle of screen direction. The term screen direction refers to the direction or movement within the frame. This direction can be created by moving or stationary people or things. This convention is very important because usually in narrative films directional continuity should be maintained from one shot to the next. The discussion of screen direction will be divided into two categories—screen direction involving motion, where people or things are moving within the frame, and static screen direction, where people and things are stationary.

The basic principle of screen direction is that things moving in a certain direction in one shot should be moving in the same direction in the next shot. Thus, a long shot of a car going left to right in the frame should be preceded or followed by a medium shot or a close-up of the car also moving left to right.

In doing this, directional continuity is maintained. The audience will believe that the car is headed in the same direction in both shots, even though this may not have been the case when the shots were filmed. If the car was going left to right in the first shot and right to left in the second shot, the audience might become disoriented. They might think that somehow the car had changed direction, and that in the second shot the car was headed in the wrong direction or in a different direction.

Screen direction can be more easily maintained by an understandiig of the *action axis principle* (also known as the 180-degree principle). The action axis principle is: To maintain proper screen direction from one shot to the next, draw an imaginary line, or action axis, through the direction that an object is moving and always keep the camera on the same side of that imaginary line (Fig. 3-8).

An important point here is that the action axis principle applies to where the axis is at the point of the cut between two shots. As the following diagram (Fig. 3–9) indicates, this can occasionally get complicated.

There are several ways to change the screen direction when things are moving in the frame. This usually involves three shots: the first shot, which shows movement in a certain direction, the second shot, which is the transition shot that changes the movement, and the third shot, which has

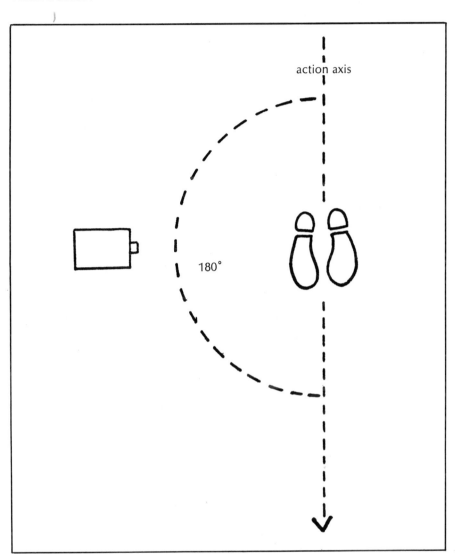

Fig. 3-8. The action axis.

the movement in an opposite direction. Conventionally, the ways of changing screen direction for moving objects or people are:

1. Using a neutral shot which is from head-on or behind the subject. The neutral shot is the transition shot (Fig. 3-10).

2. Using a character POV shot. In this instance, there is a shot of something moving in the frame from the left to right direction. This is

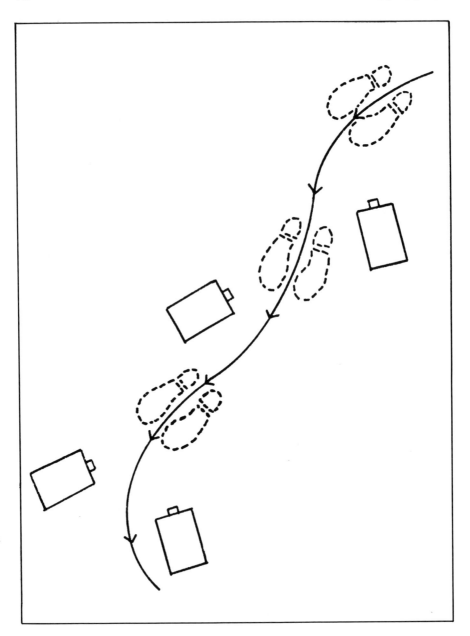

Fig. 3-9. The action axis on curves.

followed by a close-up of someone observing that movement. Next is a shot of what that person "sees." If that person is on the other side of the axis, then the screen direction will be reversed.

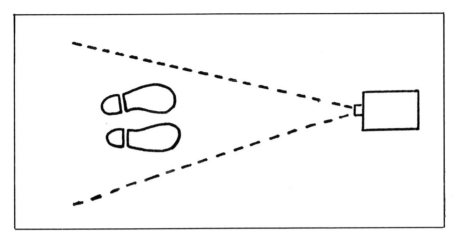

Fig. 3-10. The neutral or head-on shot for changing screen direction.

3. Movement can change direction during a shot and thereby create a new axis (Fig. 3-11).

4. The camera can cross the axis during the shot (Fig. 3-12).

Often, screen direction imitates geographical principles based on a map. Thus, if a character is flying from Los Angeles to New York and a shot of the plane in the air is included, the plane will be going in a left to right movement in the frame. In this case the frame itself is like a map. It is interesting to note that most westerns, dealing with the settling of the frontier, are characterized by a right to left screen direction. When viewing the frame like a map, this is a westerly screen direction.

Consistency with screen direction can be useful in creating spatial relationships between locations. If a script involves two locations and characters travel between those two locations, the direction of the travel from one location to another should be consistent. For example, a narrative concerns a family on a farm. They live near a small town. When the family travels from the farm to the town, they will always go in the same direction on screen. Conversely, when they come home to the farm from town, they will go in the opposite direction. By being consistent with this, audience orientation is maintained. Whenever people are seen traveling, the audience will know where they are going.

The principle of screen direction also applies when there is no movement in the frame. Again, to maintain screen direction, the action axis principle is applied. There are several basic ways of drawing the action axis when there is no directional movement in the shot.

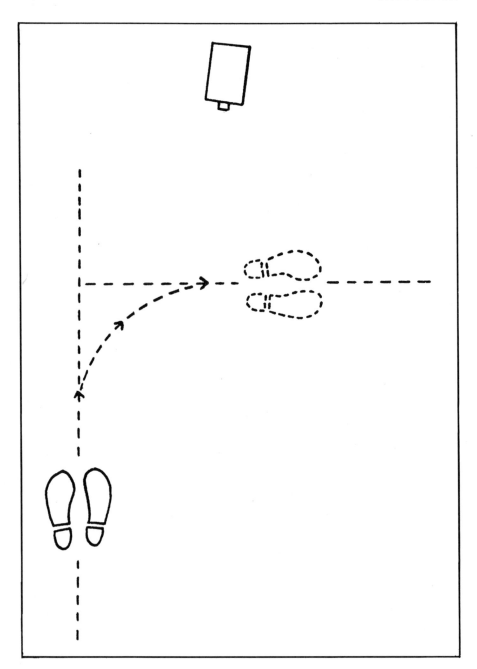

Fig. 3-11. Character movements change the action axis and therefore change screen direction.

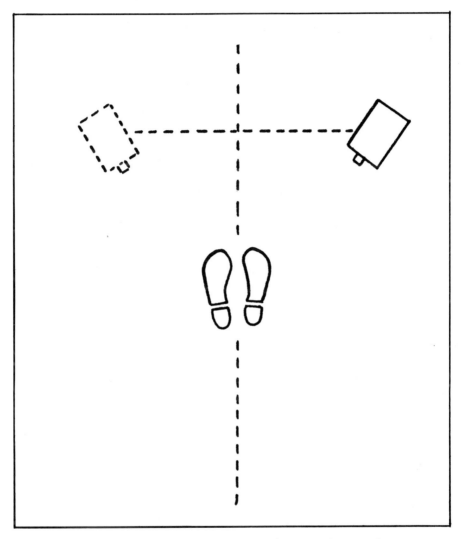

Fig. 3-12. The camera crosses the action axis during a shot to change screen direction.

The Single Person Principle. When there is only one person in the shot, the action axis is drawn from that person's perspective, and the camera will always stay on the same side of the axis (Fig. 3-13).

The reason for this is that between shots it is important to maintain character eye line continuity (the direction that a character is looking) in the frame. If the camera remains on the same side of the axis, the character will always be looking in the same direction in the frame. If the axis is crossed, the character will be looking in the opposite direction.

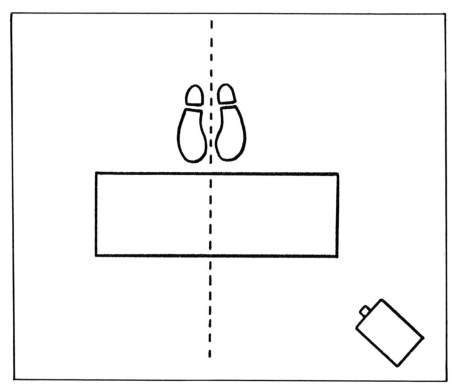

Fig. 3-13. The single person action axis principle.

The Two Person Principle. When two people are in a shot, the axis is drawn through them (Fig. 3-14). If the camera stays on the same side of the axis, character A will always be on the left side of the frame and character B on the right. Observing the action axis for shots with two people is very important when using POV shots. This maintains the notion of eye line match (Fig. 3-15).

Camera no. 3 records an objective shot and establishes that A is on the left, looking at B, and that B is on the right, looking at A. Camera no. 1 is a POV shot of B and in this shot, B will be looking right to left at A. Similarly, for camera position no. 2, A will be looking left to right at B. Thus, by cutting back and forth between no. 1 and no. 2, it is established that A and B are relating to each other. If the POV camera crosses the axis to camera position no. 4, A will be looking right to left and the shot might be disorienting and confusing.

Scenes Involving Three or More People. For scenes involving three or more people, use the one person principle or the two person principle, whichever is most applicable. For example, a wedding scene (Fig. 3-16):

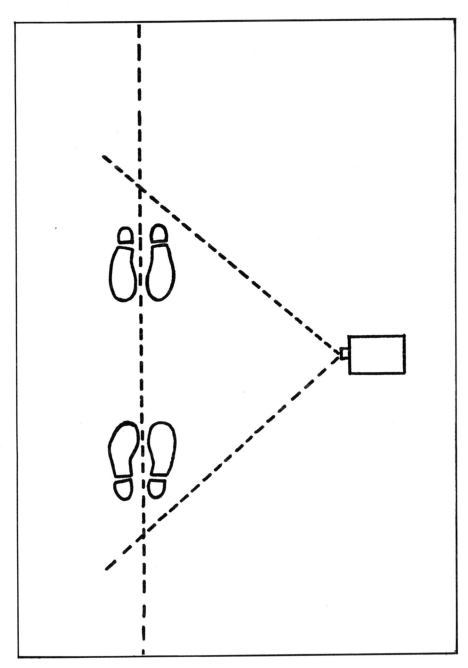

Fig. 3-14. The two person action axis principle.

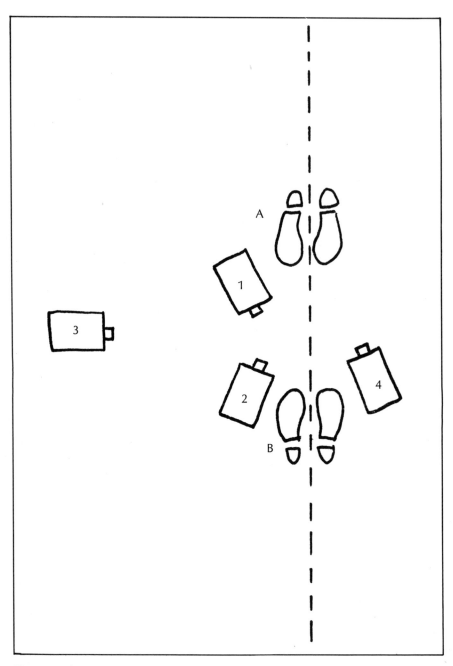

Fig. 3-15. The action axis and eye line match.

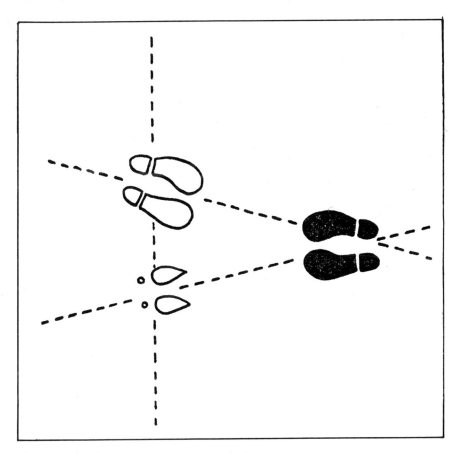

Fig. 3-16. The three person action axis principle.

In this scene, apply the principle according to the content and action within the scene and where the axis is at the point of the cut. When the preacher is speaking the wedding service, he is dominating, so apply the one person principle. When he starts to relate to either the bride or the groom, apply the two person principle and draw the axis through the preacher and either the bride or the groom. At the end of the service, when the bride and groom kiss, apply the two person principle and draw the axis through them.

The screen direction between two shots involving no movement can be changed in the following ways:

1. Character relationships can be changed within the shot, thereby changing the axis (Fig. 3-17).

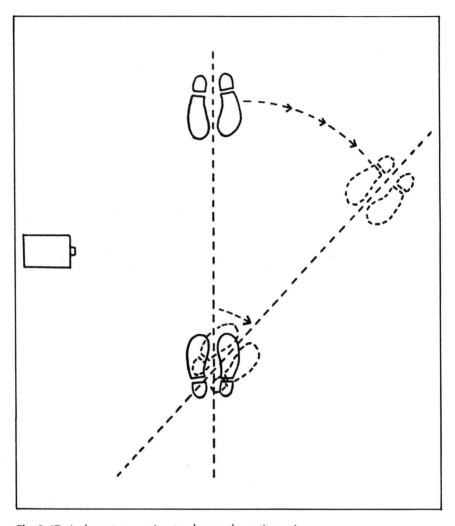

Fig. 3-17. A character moving to change the action axis.

2. The camera can cross the axis during a shot (Fig. 3-18).

3. A character POV or "seeing" shot can be used to cross the axis.

These are similar to the ways that are used to change screen direction for shots involving action or movement. The exception is a neutral camera angle. In dealing with static screen direction, a neutral shot to cross the axis is usually not employed.

The principles of screen direction and action axis discussed here are

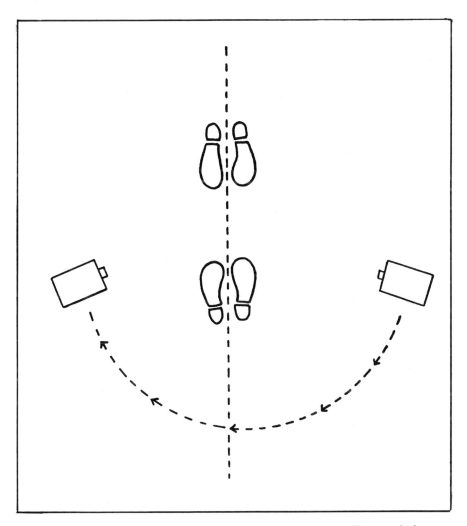

Fig. 3-18. The camera crosses the axis while two people are talking and changes screen direction.

not unbreakable rules. They are conventions and guidelines which have been developed throughout the history of motion pictures. The main function of these conventions is to make films flow, to make shots run together smoothly, and to maintain audience orientation to the action and content of the film. There are many ways in which these conventions of screen direction can be manipulated and experimented with. Because they are conventions, and therefore direct audience orientation, they can be used as tools for disorientation in terms of time and space. Thus, a conventional character POV shot might be used in the following way:

```
INTERIOR LIBRARY DAY

1. MS PAUL AND JIM ARE SEATED TALKING

        The two are both seated on chairs facing each other
        talking.

2. CU JIM FROM PAUL'S POV

        Paul is speaking and Jim seems disinterested.

3. CU PAUL FROM JIM'S POV

        Paul is getting quite animated as he speaks.

INTERIOR JIM'S APARTMENT DAY

4. CU JIM (same angle as #2) AS JIM SEEMS DISINTERESTED

        Jim is in a closeup and is apparently bored.
```

Here, shot no. 4 will initially appear to be a continuation of the inter-action between Paul and Jim. This is because the framing and camera angle for no. 4 is the same as the framing and camera angle for no. 2. Thus, initially, shot no. 4 will seem to be a POV from Paul's angle, the same as shot no. 2. The dolly back in no. 4 *reveals* the change of time and space. Stanley Donen's film, *Two for the Road*, uses this technique to great effect to create temporal and spatial transitions.

Another type of examination is possible in exploiting the implications of the character POV "seeing" shot. This experimentation is based on the convention which implies that a close-up of a character looking at something will be followed by a POV shot of what the character is seeing. Thus:

```
EXT. STREET DAY

1. MLS BILL IS WALKING DOWN A CITY STREET

        Bill is walking down a city street. Camera PANS
        with him as he walks. He stops and sees something.
```

2. CU BILL LOOKING

    Bill stops and looks at something frame left.

3. MS THE FRONT OF A STORE

    Camera HOLDS on the front of the store. In a short
    time Bill comes through the door of the store onto
    the street. He turns right and exits frame left.

Here, the first two shots prepare the audience for shot no. 3 which is, apparently, a POV "seeing" shot. Then, Bill comes out of the store and the convention is violated. Shot no. 3 is not, in fact, Bill's POV because Bill is included in this shot. Thus, a spatial and temporal transition has occurred.

There are a great many ways to use and experiment with the conventions of screen direction and eye line match. However, before any experimentation is undertaken, it is important that these conventions themselves be fully understood and appreciated.

Continuity

Good continuity, that is, precisely matched cuts, consistency in terms of props, costumes, character positioning and lighting, can be better maintained if a continuity log is kept during shooting. Below is a sample continuity log which takes these factors into consideration (Fig. 3-19).

Lighting

One of the most important and one of the most difficult aspects of filmmaking is lighting. This is particularly difficult on the level of independent and student filmmaking because of the inaccessibility of sophisticated lighting units and studios. In this section on lighting, we will discuss some

SCENE LOG—CONTINUITY   DATE_____

SEQUENCE	SHOT	TAKE	PRINT	PICTURE	TIME OF SHOT	SOUND

Fig. 3-19. A sample continuity log.

of the theories and techniques of lighting in professional filmmaking and apply these to the problems of independent and student filmmaking.

A light has essentially three properties—intensity, directionality and characteristic. The intensity of a light refers to its brightness, and in lighting units this is measured in watts. In amateur work, a 1000w light is a very powerful source. Normally, one uses photofloods (200–500w) or movie lights (500–600w). In professional filmmaking studios, it is common to find lighting units as powerful as 5000w or 10000w. A primary consideration in terms of lighting intensity should be simply to use a lighting unit or units which have sufficient brightness to permit shooting. Shooting with Kodachrome 40 will necessitate lights of greater intensity than shooting with Ektachrome (160), so in choosing a film stock the lighting equipment available should be considered. Speaking of lighting intensity, it is important to note that camera exposure (f-stop) never varies as the camera moves closer or farther away from the subject, but exposure does change as the light is moved closer or farther away from the subject (Fig. 3-20).

Lighting directionality refers to the direction a light is coming from in relation to the subject. When filming people, there are two planes of lighting directionality to consider, the horizontality to consider, the horizontal and the vertical. These planes are broken down as follows:

1. *Horizontal*—back, ¾ back, side, ¾ front and front

2. *Vertical*—top, 45 degree, eye level, low angle

In general, these variations in lighting direction have come to suggest a variety of things to an audience. Again, bear in mind that these are conventions, not rules. They are the way in which filmmakers in general have come to use film techniques and audiences have come to understand them. They exist to be violated after you have understood and used them.

1. *Horizontal*:
    (A) Back, ¾ back and side—mystery, drama, tension

    (B) ¾ front—strong character

    (C) Front—less interesting character

2. *Vertical*:
    (A) Top—uninteresting, bland

    (B) 45 degree—strong, interesting character

    (C) Eye level—less interesting character

    (D) Low angle—wicked, often used in horror films

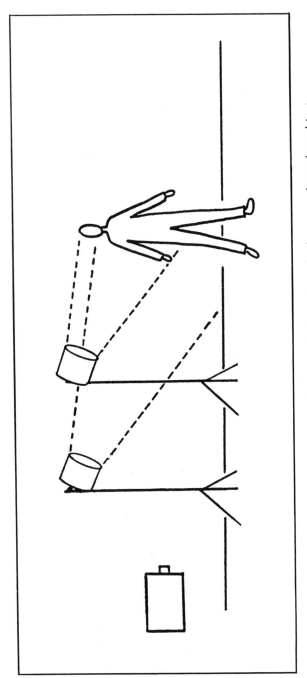

Fig. 3-20. Exposure changes greatly as a lighting unit is moved closer to or further away from the subject.

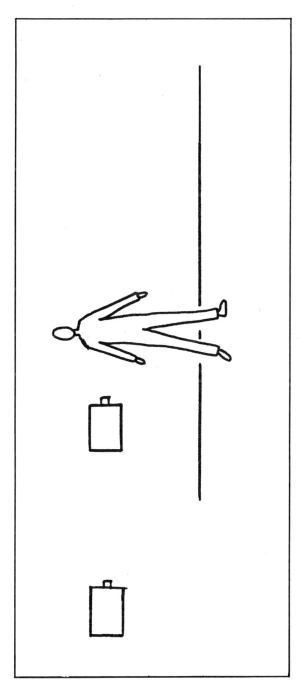

Fig. 3-20. (Continued) There is no change in exposure as camera to subject distance is changed.

Back lighting.

¾ back lighting.

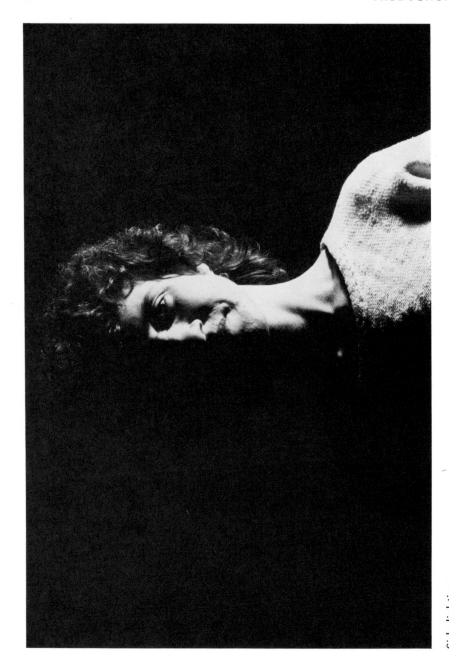

Side lighting.

³/₄ front lighting.

Front lighting.

Low angle lighting.

Lighting characteristic is probably the most difficult property of light to understand. Characteristic refers to the quality of light as it hits the subject. This is usually discussed in terms of *harsh* and *soft* lighting. A light with a harsh characteristic creates hard, dark shadows and shadow areas. Harsh lighting is usually the result of using open faced lighting units, such as photofloods, quartz lights and movie lights. Shown in the photo example, harsh lighting in portraits and close ups renders faces with hard shadows and high contrast—a generally displeasing effect. A central consideration in lighting, then, is to soften the light. This means to make its characteristic softer, soften the shadows, and lower the contrast between dark and light areas. This is accomplished in a variety of ways. The most common way is to diffuse the lighting source by placing diffusion material between the lighting unit and the subject. Diffusion materials change the characteristic of the light or soften it.

Common diffusion materials are spun glass and Tuff-spun (brand name). These can be purchased at professional camera stores. It is possible to devise a homemade diffusion material, but these may burn if the material is placed too close to the lighting unit. This is the major reason for using commercial diffusing products, as they are nonflammable and can be placed quite close to the lamp. Household materials that are good for diffusion are clear or white shower curtains, frosted glass, and frosted Plexiglas (trademark). Again, be careful not to place these materials too close to the lamp of the lighting units.

Another common way of softening light is using indirect or bounced light. Using this method, a light is bounced or reflected off of a surface which diffuses it onto the subject. Common practice in still photography is to use reflector umbrellas. A light is pointed toward a reflector which is umbrella shaped. The light reflecting off of the umbrella is very soft because of the matte surface inside the umbrella. In lighting for movies, good results can often be obtained by bouncing light off of a ceiling or wall and onto the subject. White or light colored walls work best as they reflect the greatest amount of light. An important point here is to remember that the angle of incidence equals the angle of reflection; so to get the greatest amount of reflection on the subject, the angle that the light is hitting the reflected surface must be controlled and directed (Fig. 3-21).

Having discussed these three properties of light, we now move to a discussion of basic lighting set-ups. In studio lighting, there are three basic functions for lighting units. These are called the *key* light, the *fill* light and the *back* light.

The key light is that lighting unit which is the primary source of illumination for the subject. The key light is usually quite directional; it is pointed directly at the subject and does not spill onto unwanted areas. Key lights are usually placed above eye level—45 degrees is best. This

Harsh lighting.

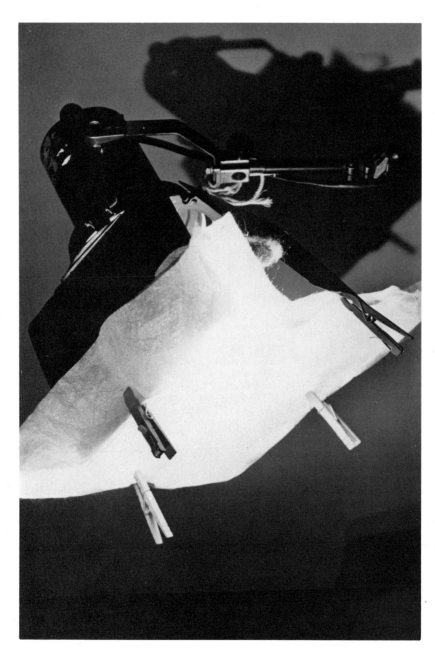

A lighting unit diffused with spun glass.

A bounce light set-up.

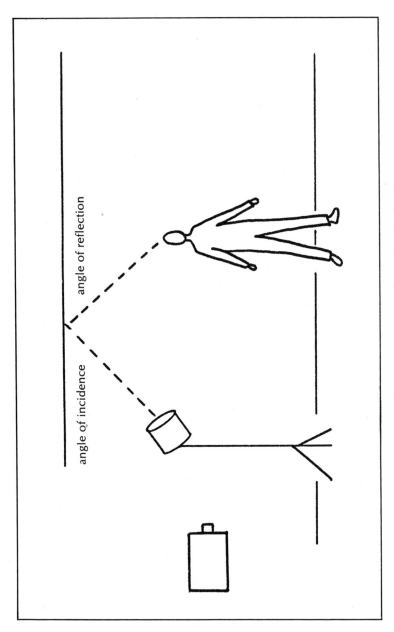

Fig. 3-21. In bounce lighting, the angle of incidence equals the angle of reflection.

makes facial shadows more pleasing and makes the actors more comfortable because the lights are above their angle of view.

The fill light is that light which is used to illuminate the subject and the area around the subject. It is placed at eye level and on the opposite side of the camera from the key light. It is usually a very diffused, soft light so that it creates a minimum of shadows.

The back light is placed above and behind the subject. This is pointed directly at the top and back of the actor's head and is used to create a rim light on the head and shoulders. The back light adds depth to the image, as it helps separate the subject from the background.

There are general guidelines for the relative intensities of the key, fill, and back lights. For color films, the ratio is usually that the key is twice as intense as the back and fill. So, if a 1000w key light is being used, the fill and back should be 500w each. All three should be of equal distance from the subject. For black and white filming, this ratio is often higher. For example, the key can be 1000w, the fill 250w, and the back 500w. As this key-to-fill ratio goes up, the relative contrast of the scene increases. Thus, in the second example (key=1000w, fill=250w) the subject would be considerably brighter than the surrounding area, and there would be darker shadows on the subject's face.

In most location shooting situations, there will not be enough lighting units to create key, back, and fill lighting as described above. In these cases, available light sources can be used as these types of light. For example, a scene is being shot at a friend's house. The scene takes place in the living room and includes someone reading a book on a couch. The only lighting equipment available is one movie light and one photoflood, plus the lamps at the friend's house. In this example, a possible lighting set-up might be: Use a household lamp as a key light (this is a logical "key source"), suspend the photoflood (diffused with spun glass) above and slightly behind the subject, and use a movie light as a bounce fill light off the ceiling. The lit scene should be analyzed by looking through the camera. The consideration here is one of contrast or key-to-fill ratio. If the key, the household lamp, does not seem bright enough, use a stronger bulb, possibly a 150w as opposed to a 75w bulb, to make the scene brighter.

Some general suggestions for interior lighting are:

1. Avoid direct lighting with open faced lighting units. Diffused or soft light is more pleasing.

2. Avoid shooting in rooms with very white or light colored walls. These tend to wash out on the film and make scenes look stark and cold. In framing, use white walls for bounce but shoot against dark colored walls.

A key, back and fill set-up.

3. Avoid using too much light. Shadows and dark areas will make a film more interesting. Very bright scenes, where everything is visible, are less interesting.

4. For color films, be careful when mixing daylight (through a window, for example) and artificial light. As is described later in this chapter, the film will render poor colors if the two are mixed.

5. If a special light is to be used as a key light, make sure it comes from a logical direction. That is, its direction should be suggested by some part of the scene—a table lamp, a window, or a partially open door. If the key light is coming from no logical direction, the lighting will look artificial and contrived.

6. Be aware of and careful of highly reflective surfaces in a shot. These can be picked up on the film and can be very distracting. For example, shiny table tops, dishes, and glass table tops can create reflections. To avoid reflection, change the angle of the light so the reflection is not picked up through the lens.

Shooting outdoors presents special problems which are related to the points made about indoor shooting and lighting. The first problem in outdoor shooting is the sun, which is a very bright, harsh, key light. The sun usually casts very harsh and displeasing shadows. Therefore, the old rule for photography which says, "Always shoot with the sun over your shoulder," is, for all practical purposes, wrong. This rule originated in the early days of still photography, when the fastest films had an ASA of 6 and the fastest lenses were f-11. Consequently, it was necessary to have the sun over your shoulder in order to have enough light on the subject. Today, these factors of exposure are no longer a consideration. Outdoor visuals will be more pleasing if the sun is not shining directly on an actor's face. Therefore, try to shoot in such a way that the sun is not shining directly on an actor. This will help eliminate some of the harsh quality of direct sunlight. Another problem when shooting outside is the great difference in proper exposure between sunlit areas and shaded areas. This can sometimes amount to as much as a two f-stop difference in exposure. This means that if a shot includes someone sitting in the shade, the area surrounding the shaded area, that area in sunlight, will be quite overexposed. The reverse also holds true. Exposure for sunlit areas will render shaded areas underexposed. Therefore, avoid including both sunlit areas and shaded areas in the same shot. These two problems, the problem of direct sunlight and the problem of shaded areas and brightly lit areas, are not a factor when shooting on a cloudy or overcast day. Therefore, better visual results are often possible when shooting on overcast days. However, an overcast sky often responds like a white wall in an interior. Images will tend to appear washed out and stark if too much sky is included in the shot. In summary:

1. On sunny days, avoid shooting with direct sunlight on an actor's face. Instead, try to position the camera and actor so that the sun is above and behind the actor. Also avoid including shaded areas and brightly sunlit areas in the same shot. Here, exposure will always be a problem.

2. On overcast days, try to keep a light, overcast sky out of the shot. This will usually entail a higher camera angle in order to keep the sky out of the shot.

Color Filming

Color films, unlike black and white films, have to be matched or "balanced" for particular shooting situations. Black and white films, like Plus-X or Tri-X, can be shot either outdoors or indoors. As discussed in Chapter 1, it is advisable, because of ASA ratings, to shoot Plus-X outdoors and Tri-X indoors, but this is only a suggestion. If the situation demanded it, one could shoot Tri-X outdoors and Plus-X indoors. However, this is not the case with color films. All color films are balanced for either indoor shooting (lighting) conditions or outdoor shooting conditions. The reasons for this is that there is a difference in the color "balance" between indoor and outdoor light. Light in its purest state is made up of three primary colors, red, blue, and green. Outdoor light is a kind of light that represents a fairly accurate balance between red, blue and green. The sun, which is the primary light source outdoors, emits a fairly balanced type of light. A film stock which is balanced or matched for outdoor light also has a fairly even response to red, blue, and green. The result will be proper color on the film.

Indoor light is not balanced in terms of red, blue and green. In fact, indoor light, which is usually created by tungsten lamps (normal household lights), is reddish. One's eyes usually cannot detect this because they compensate almost instantaneously to make color seem balanced and normal. Color films do not have the ability to compensate as the eyes do. They must be properly balanced for a particular shooting situation, either indoors or outdoors. Thus, there are essentially two types of color films; there are outdoor color films, often called daylight films (or type D), and indoor films (called type A and sometimes type B). An outdoor color film has a color-sensitive emulsion which is equally sensitive to red, blue, and green light, and when this film is shot outdoors, it will render colors normally. An indoor color film has an emulsion which is very sensitive to blue and green, but not very sensitive to red. This is to compensate for the excess amount of red light in most indoor lighting situations. Different color films are balanced for different lighting situations. It is possible to use an indoor balanced film outdoors; it is common practice in Super-8 filmmaking. This can be done if the camera is equipped with a conversion filter, usually referred to as an 85 filter. This amber filter "converts" indoor films (Type A or B) to outdoor conditions. It does this by filtering or rebalancing the indoor emulsion, which is more blue sensitive than red sensitive, to normal balanced outdoor conditions. Virtually all Super-8 cameras have an indoor/outdoor selector switch or filter pin for use with indoor color films. In the "indoor" position (with filter pin in place) the 85 filter is not in place in front of the film plane. In the "outdoor" position (filter pin removed) the filter comes into place for the conversion.

The principle of color balance applies to lights as well as film stocks. In other words, indoor color film is balanced for a particular type of indoor light. Good results are not possible by simply shooting color films indoors using normal room lights. Color film is balanced for a particular type of light. Type A indoor films are designed to be shot while using what are referred to as 3400°K (K=Kelvin, a fixed unit for measuring light) lights. This means that when shooting with Type A film (Kodachrome 40), a no. 1 BBA or no. 2 EBV photoflood or a 3400° Kelvin quartz or movie light should be used. If a Type B indoor film (Ektachrome EF) is the film stock, best color results will be obtained by using 3200°K photofloods or 3200°K quartz lights or movie lights. In practice, Types A and B films can be used interchangeably with either 3400°K or 3200°K lights, because the color balance difference is very small. But both of these films will yield very poor results when shot while using home tungsten lights (household lamps or overhead lights, etc.). An important point is that these two films render colors very poorly when shot under fluorescent lighting conditions. Fluorescent lights usually emit a predominantly green color. The result is that color film shot under fluorescent lighting usually has a very pale green tint. Therefore, whenever possible, avoid shooting color in fluorescent lighting situations. There is a filter available which makes it possible to shoot film under fluorescent lights. This is called the FLB filter, and with it good results are possible. It is advisable, however, to film tests with this filter at the shooting location before it is used in an actual filming situation.

These then, are the basic rules and principles of color filming. If the principles of color balance are understood and observed, working with color films is quite easy and good color results can be expected.

4 Post-Production

The first section of this chapter will deal with film editing and will be divided into two parts. The first part will deal with the mechanics of film editing and the second part will be an introduction to the theory and esthetics of film editing.

Before going into the basic techniques and tools of editing, it is necessary to understand some basic principles about the film generational process. By the generational process, we mean the ways in which all professional (and some independent and amateur) films are shot and edited, and then how several or a great many prints of the film are released in distribution. In the making of most feature films, documentaries, commercials, and educational films, the following is common practice.

Film Generations

The film shot in the camera is called *camera original*. It is a very valuable material as it is the only record of what was filmed. If it is scratched, torn, or broken, then this record is permanently damaged. Because of this, great care must be taken to protect and preserve the original. This is the basis for the film generational process. Under professional circumstances, the camera original is exposed in the camera and then processed by the lab. Then, a duplicate or copy of the original is made. This is called a *work-print*. This workprint is a frame by frame copy of the original. The workprint is then used for editing purposes. It is spliced, re-spliced, and run through projectors and viewers. During the editing process, the original from which the workprint was made is stored safely away and neither projected nor edited. When the workprint is completely edited, or at a *fine cut* stage, then it becomes time to refer to the originals. Based on the workprint, the camera originals are edited or *conformed* to the editing in the workprint. One does this conforming process with great care, using white gloves and a clean editing bench. Every precaution must be taken while handling the original. When the originals have been conformed to the workprint, they are sent to the lab and prints are made from them. Thus, multiple prints of the film can be made and distributed. Again, the originals are never subjected to being scratched or torn. They are never projected or run through a viewer. The workprint serves the function its name implies; it is used for editing and working purposes only. Once the originals have been conformed to the fine cut workprint and prints have been made, the workprint has served its purpose and is henceforth useless.

The above is actually an extreme simplification of the generational process. In practice, the conforming process for the originals is quite complex, as is the process whereby prints are made. But the important point here is the distinction between originals, workprints, and final prints.

In most Super-8 filmmaking, workprints and final prints are not made. The original is simply shot and then edited into what is to become the final film. Therefore, a primary concern in Super-8 editing should be taking care of the film. It is the camera original, the only record. Common practice in Super-8 filmmaking is to carefully edit the original, and then a print or prints can be made directly from it. This is an especially good idea if the film is to be shown a great many times—in festivals, or for school or job applications. Prints can be shown and the originals preserved. In most large cities, 16mm film labs now offer Super-8 printing services.

The Mechanics of Film Editing

The basic tools in film editing are the viewer, the rewinds, the splicer, and the projector. Most viewers come with rewind arms attached, and well-known brands are Vernon, Baia, Minette, and Moviescop (this last requires a separate, table-mounted rewind). There are two types of splicers on the market—the tape splicer and the cement splicer. Most tape splicers work on a butt splice system. That is, the two pieces of film are butted up to one another at the frame line. If two shots joined by a tape splice are to be changed, it is simply a matter of removing the tape and adding or subtracting the desired number of frames. Then, re-splice at the same point. The cement splice works on an overlapping principle. At the point where the splice is made, the two pieces of film are overlapped slightly to provide an area for the cement bonding. This overlap occurs partially in the viewable frame area, meaning that the splice will be quite visible when projected. Tape splices are also visible when projected. The tape on the film can be seen as the splice goes by but less so than cement splices. Another major drawback to the cement splice is that in order to create the overlap, a frame of film must be destroyed; a portion

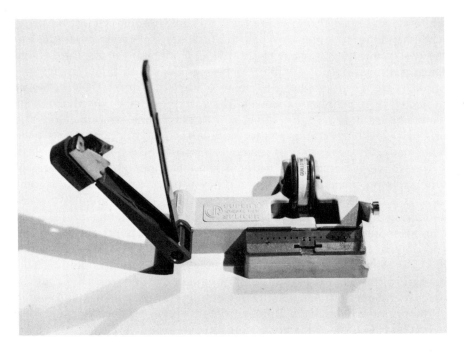

Super-8 tape splicer.

of one frame provides the necessary area for the overlap. So, to change the splice after making a cement splice is very difficult. Frames cannot be added or subtracted. The frames adjoining the splice have been cut to provide the overlap. This is an especially important consideration when editing originals.

The viewer can be used to make decisions as to where and how to cut two shots together. However, it is very difficult to determine the proper length of shots and the timing and pacing of sequences on a viewer. This is because it is difficult to hand crank rewinds at a consistent speed and thereby gauge the proper rhythm that scenes or sequences should have. Therefore, a good practice is to loosely edit the shots together. This is called an assemblage. Then, project the assemblage onto a screen several times, and in the process try to determine at what precise points edits should be made. Now, go back to the viewer and cut down the assemblage into a *rough cut*, which means that the film is roughly cut together but not yet precisely timed and paced. Then project the film again, this time thinking in terms of a *fine cut*—the fully edited version of the film. It is with the projector that decisions are made and with the viewer that these decisions are executed. This is true not only because of the hand cranking problem but because one's perceptions of what looks good on a small

Super-8 cement splicer.

viewer screen can be misleading. A cut that seems to work when cranked through a viewer may often appear jarring or disorienting when projected on a screen.

Some tips on the mechanics of film editing:

1. Always work in a clean editing area—dirt on film creates scratches.

2. Make many practice splices on leader or outtakes before actually splicing your film.

3. Inspect all splices carefully before projecting your film. A faulty splice can get jammed in the projector and cause broken sprocket holes and/or film.

4. Keep your projector and viewer clean.

5. Handle the film as little as possible. In fact, it is advisable to use editing gloves.

6. Use plenty of leader at the head and tail of your film.

7. Never let your film fall on the floor or slide across the editing table.

A 16mm editing bench.

A 16mm horizontal motorized editor, the Moviola M-77.

8. Never show your film on a projector that is unfamiliar to you. You may thread it wrong and damage your film, or the projector may scratch your film and you will not find out until it is too late.

9. Never "cinch" your film. This means pulling it too tight on a reel or trying to make a loosely wound reel tighter by pulling up the slack. This will make the film rub together throughout the entire reel and will cause bad scratches.

10. If a sprocket hole does get torn, or the film breaks, use a tape splice to repair it. Never project a film with damaged sprocket holes. You run the risk of having the film jam in the projector and more sprockets will be damaged or the film will break.

11. Occasionally clean your film with a commercial film cleaner and a cotton glove or cloth. Do not clean it too often as this may cause scratches or cause your tape splices to loosen up.

12. Tape down the ends of your film when it is on a reel. This will prevent the film from becoming loose on the reel and therefore, it will prevent cinching.

13. When you are making your assemblage, you may hang your shots on the wall or in an editing bin. Always label shots clearly with paper tape or masking tape. This will save time in splicing together the assemblage. Also, carefully label all outtakes. You may find yourself needing them at the later stage in the editing process.

14. When projecting an assemblage or rough cut, take notes as to the decisions you make.

Theories and Esthetics of Editing

On a very basic level, styles of editing can be divided into two areas—invisible editing and emphatic editing. Invisible editing implies a style of editing which seeks to hide or conceal the edits, and to make the film flow. This style is usually geared toward the preservation of the illusion of reality within the film. Cuts are smooth, the film flows, and the main function of this style of editing is to make the cuts themselves as unjarring and as invisible as possible. Emphatic editing has the opposite function. This style of editing seeks to draw attention to the juxtaposition between two shots, rather than conceal this juxtaposition. There are no concrete rules as to when one would choose one style over the other. They are often mixed within a film. There will be a further discussion of this question after an examination of the two styles.

Because invisible editing seeks to conceal the editing process and preserve an illusion, there are several conventions which have evolved to meet this end. The first is the principle of match cut. The match cut is a cut which involves matching action within a scene. For example:

```
1.   MS JOHN TALKING TO BILL

2.   CU JOHN TALKING TO BILL
```

This is a match cut. John must be in the same position between shots no. 1 and no. 2. If he is not in exactly the same position, the cut will be jarring. John will appear to jump or move between the shots. Match cuts are very difficult to execute. In the example above, John's action and position in the camera placement for shot no. 1 must be matched with John's action and position in the camera placement for shot no. 2.

Given the time it takes to move the camera, re-set the lights and set up a shot, this can be very difficult. There are several conventions for making match cuts. The first convention is to match cut, wherever possible, on motion or movement. When cutting on character movement, the movement itself tends to conceal the edit. This principle can be seen at work in most fight scenes. The cuts often occur on motion within the fight and therefore, the editing within the fight scene appears to flow. The actual change from one shot to another goes unnoticed because the eyes were following the motion. This, of course, only works if the two shots are matched in terms of the action.

A second convention for smooth match cutting is to change camera angle for a cut by at least 30°, or focal length by at least 10mm, or both. By observing either of these two suggestions, both of which will make the framing between the two shots significantly different, the cut will be more successful. A camera position change of less than 30° will result in only a slight framing change and the cut may seem jumpy or jarring. A move of 30° or more presents new information in the shot, making the cut more explicit. The same holds true for a change in focal length of less than 10mm. In any match cutting situation, the principles of action axis and screen direction should be considered.

Another invisible editing convention involves the use of entrances and exits. These can be especially useful in condensing film time in terms of real time. The principle of this convention is to have a character exit frame in one shot and enter frame in the next. To maintain screen direction, the character's entrance should be on the opposite side of the frame from his exit. For example:

```
EXT. CITY STREET

1.  MS BILL GETS INTO HIS CAR AND DRIVES OFF


    BILL opens his car door, starts the car and the car
    exits frame left.

EXT. SUBURBAN STREET

2. MLS BILL'S HOUSE FROM THE OTHER SIDE OF THE STREET

   BILL'S car enters from frame right and pulls into the driveway.
```

In this example, film time has been condensed in terms of real time. Bill actually drove from the city to his house. The exits and entrances in the shots make the transition between the shots smooth and create the illusion that Bill actually did drive from the city to his home, without this event being shown in the film. It is sometimes possible to cut together two shots, the first of which has a character exit while the second picks up the action at a new location without an entrance:

```
EXT. CITY STREET

1. MS BILL GETS INTO HIS CAR AND DRIVES OFF

   BILL opens his car door, starts the car and the car exits
   frame left.

EXT. SUBURBAN STREET

2. MS BILL'S CAR IS PULLING INTO THE DRIVEWAY
```

In this instance, the first shot has Bill's car exiting the frame. The second shot picks up the action as Bill's car is in the driveway. There is no entrance. In all likelihood, the entrance would be shot; then it becomes an editorial decision as to whether to leave it in or not. In shooting, it is always good practice to include character entrances and exits whenever possible. This will always make editing easier.

Another invisible editing convention which helps condense film time versus real time is the cut-in. A cut-in is usually a close-up portion of a scene. The cut-in can be used as follows:

```
INT. OFFICE

1. MS JOHN AT TYPEWRITER (20 sec)

   JOHN feeds a piece of paper into the typewriter and begins
   typing a letter

2. CU THE TYPEWRITER KEYS (7 sec)

   JOHN is typing.

3. MS JOHN FINISHING THE LETTER (15 sec)

   JOHN types the last few words and rolls the finished letter
   out of the typewriter carriage.
```

In this example, shot no. 2 is a cut-in. The total screen time for these three shots would probably be 30–45 seconds, yet the entire action of John typing the letter may, in real time, have taken five minutes. The cut-in provides the bridge for the condensation of time. The audience will accept the fact that a certain amount of action took place between the cuts—the edit from shot no. 2 to shot no. 3. The cut-in, therefore, can be a very valuable filmic tool. With it, a great deal of action and business can be shown in a relatively short period of time. Other uses of the cut-in might be:

```
INT. OFFICE

1. MS MARY AT PHONE

   MARY picks up the receiver and begins to dial a number.

2. CU PHONE

   MARY'S fingers dial the number

3. MS MARY

   She begins talking to a friend on the phone.
```

Here, the time-consuming process of dialing seven numbers can be condensed by the use of the cut-in. Another example:

```
      EXT. STREET

   1. MLS BILL GETTING INTO HIS CAR

      BILL opens the car door and gets into the car.

   2. CU CAR KEY TURNING IN THE IGNITION

      BILL starts the car.

   3. MS BILL'S CAR PULLING AWAY

      The car pulls away and exits frame left.
```

In summary, the basic principles of invisible editing are match cutting by cutting on movement and changing camera angle and/or lens, using exits and entrances, and using cut-ins.

Emphatic editing serves an entirely different function from invisible editing. With emphatic editing, one seeks to emphasize the juxtaposition between two shots and draw the audience's attention to this juxtaposition, rather than hide it. There are several emphatic editing conventions. The first of these is cross cutting. Cross cutting is a way of developing a narrative by cutting back and forth between two different events, characters or locations. By convention, cross cutting virtually demands that the two disparate actions which have been cross cut come together at some point in the film. Cross cutting is used in many chase scenes. In chase scenes, the pursued and the pursuer are cross cut. Consider, for example, a criminal being chased by a posse. The criminal crosses a narrow bridge and in the next shot, the posse crosses the narrow bridge. The criminal crosses a small stream and the posse crosses a small stream and so forth. This kind of cross cutting emphasizes the relationship between the criminal and the posse. This relationship builds until the criminal is finally caught.

Another type of emphatic editing is the use of the associational or relational cut. An association cut is an edit between two shots in which there is a relation or association. This relation or similarity can be in terms of form, movement, color or idea. An example of a relational cut is the following:

```
      INT. OFFICE

   1. CU JOHN TYPING

   2. CU BILL DRUMMING HIS FINGERS ON A DESK
```

Here, there is a relation between form and movement. Another example:

```
    EXT. YARD

  1. MS JOHN SAWING A BOARD IN HALF

    INT. KITCHEN

  2. MARY CARVING A TURKEY
```

Here, the relationship is based on movement and action, both people are cutting something. A more complex associational edit would be:

```
  1. LS LOW ANGLE OF A STRING OF ELECTRICAL WIRES

  2. CU GUITAR STRINGS AS SOMEONE IS PLAYING A GUITAR
```

Here, the relationship is based on form only. The form of the first shot is similar to the form of the second.

A variation on the relational edit is a type of edit where the two shots joined together suggest opposition or antithesis in terms of the ideas conveyed. A shot of migrant workers cut together with a shot of a political banquet would be an example of this type of edit. Sometimes this is called "collision editing," as the two shots, being so radically different in idea, collide on the screen.

The final kind of emphatic cut is the jump cut. A jump cut is a type of edit which jarringly portrays a leap forward in time, usually a short period of time, but not always so. Thus a jump cut would be:

```
    INT. BATHROOM

  1. MS JOHN BRUSHING HIS TEETH

  2. MS(SAME CAMERA POSITION) JOHN COMBING HIS HAIR
```

Here, there has been a bridge of time. The real time that John took to finish brushing his teeth and took to begin combing his hair has been cut out, but the camera angle stayed the same between the cuts. The jump cut is a very jarring filmic device. It emphatically breaks up any illusion of reality and by doing so, draws attention to itself and to the time gap that has been created. Jump cuts usually work best if the same precise camera angle and lens are used between the two shots. This will make it very clear that the jump cut is intentional. If the intent is not clear, the cut may seem to be a technical error; it may seem, simply, to be a bad match cut.

As was mentioned earlier, it is difficult to state precisely when either an invisible editing style or an emphatic editing style is called for. In many films, the two styles are combined. A film like *Bonnie and Clyde*, for example, utilizes invisible editing for most of the sequences which develop the narrative. Yet in certain sequences, emphatic editing techniques are used—the cross cutting in the chase sequences and the final close-up cross cutting between Bonnie and Clyde as they are ambushed at the end of the film. These two styles can even be mixed together on the same cut. It is possible to create a cut which is essentially invisible and at the same time, has associational elements in terms of form, movement or idea.

In general, invisible editing implies less editing than emphatic editing in terms of the actual number of cuts. Invisible is functional and relies on the action within the scene to convey a message. Emphatic editing seeks to generate more than is actually in the scene by the juxtaposition of shots. Invisible editing techniques generally are used to develop a narrative smoothly and efficiently and to sustain an illusion of reality. Emphatic editing techniques are used to punctuate or emphasize certain elements and relations in a shot or scene; emphatic edits can intensify action or conflict and create a synthesis from the juxtaposition of two shots or scenes which suggest ideas.

The disadvantages or pitfalls of the two styles are that, at its worst, invisible editing can be work-a-day, bland, and unimaginative. Emphatic editing can be heavy-handed, lack subtlety, and be jarring.

There are sometimes instances when a film can be constructed in the editing process. This is usually the case with a verité documentary. A great deal of footage is shot and the film is then scripted in the editing room from the footage. The film should still have been shot, however, with the basic principles of editing in mind. A key to shooting for editing in instances like this would be to shoot character reaction shots or cut-aways and cut-ins. Having a great many reaction shots will make for editing flexibility. A reaction shot can be used to bridge a poor match or change in time. Intercutting reaction shots will help the film flow.

The most important point we can make in this section on editing is that film editing is an integral part of the filmmaking process, along with scripting and shooting. All three must work together. The old saying,

"We'll save it in the editing room," just does not hold true for any type of filmmaking. If two shots do not match cut or a relational edit does not work, there is no way of saving it. But shots with match cut and associated edits will work if careful considerations are made in the scripting and shooting process.

Silence or Sound

The question of silent film or sound film is not a "which came first" issue. In the United States, sound was clearly first. Thomas Edison urged his staff to develop a moving picture so he could sell more "talking machines." Edison's idea was to give the public something to look at while they listened to the music on his invention—the sound talking machine.

Sound accompaniment to film came early in film history. But technical problems and the popularity of the moving picture itself caused early filmmakers to turn almost exclusively to silent pictures. However, "silent" films were not completely silent. From the first nickelodeons to the coming of sound in 1927, musical accompaniment for film was provided by a piano player or orchestra. Most of the music played was written specifically for the film being shown. Enterprising theaters also employed sound effects men, and pianists often tried to duplicate or suggest sound effects.

The silent film did develop as a kind of special case with special conventions, however. Since the characters could not speak, the filmmaker had two choices. The filmmaker either worked around the need for words, or titles were made to indicate what people were saying. Even with titles, the movies had to remain essentially non-dialogue presentations, or the audience would be overwhelmed by written words. Therefore, the silent movies developed techniques which carried on into sound films. The close-up was, in part, a result of silence and the need to get near the face, which might reveal what the voice could not. A tendency toward action that did not require dialogue was also marked in American silent films.

The choice of the filmmaker is not so simple now. The means for using sound are available, whether it be as simple as making a cassette recording of music or sound effects to go with the film, or engaging in the work of making the film a sync sound production. Today, if one decides not to use sound, there should be a good reason for it and there are very few good reasons. Even if the filmmaker wishes to duplicate the aura of the silent film comedy or melodrama, there is the expectation of music. This expectation existed from the earliest days of film. Probably the only excuse for not using sound today is that the equipment for recording and reproducing sound is not available. If the decision to make a totally silent film is made, it should be for this reason and this reason only. But it must be realized that this is almost always a deficiency, not a virtue.

Sound Generations

There is a generational process that applies to film sound as well as film images. In professional filmmaking, there are two basic ways of recording sound and picture. These are single system and double system recording. Single system involves a process whereby the sound is recorded directly onto a magnetic stripe on the film as it is run through the camera. This is accomplished by way of a sound recording module in the camera. The sound and picture are recorded in the same machine—the single system camera. The advantage to this system is that instant lip sync sound is possible. After the sound striped film is processed, the synchronized sound and picture can be projected on a magnetic sound projector. The disadvantage is that it is very difficult to edit film shot in this manner. This is because of picture-sound separation. In this system, the sound is recorded advanced from the picture and is played back on a system with the same advance. In 16mm magnetic sound, this advance is 28 frames (26 frames for optical sound). In Super-8, this advance is 18 frames. Thus, to cut or edit the film means that if the cut is made at the proper point in the sound track, the visuals will be cut too early. Or, if the visuals are cut at the proper point, the sound will be cut too late.

Single system is used in both 16mm and Super-8, but because of the problems in editing, its application is very limited. In 16mm, single system is primarily used for newsfilm recording (ENG, or video news recording, has virtually made 16mm newsfilm obsolete). Speed and simplicity are of foremost importance here and single system offers this. In Super-8, single system is now used for sound home movies and for educational and industrial applications of Super-8. Aside from special applications involving speed and/or simplicity, single system recording is limited.

Double system recording is what its name implies; it is a double system whereby the picture is recorded in the camera and the sound is recorded on a separate machine. The picture and sound are kept separate until the final printing process (Fig. 4-1). The generational process for sound in double system recording is:

1. Original recording is made on ¼-inch tape or cassette.

2. Original recording is dubbed (copied) onto magnetic full coat filmstock which is the same gauge as the picture.

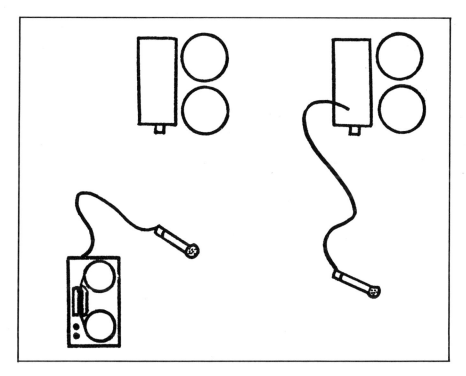

Fig. 4-1. Single system and double system film and sound recording.

3. The picture and sound are edited together as both are now on sprocketed material which can be synced.

4. The edited and/or mixed sound track on magnetic sound film is dubbed onto an optical film track in 16mm. It usually remains on magnetic stock in Super-8.

5. The optical film track is printed onto the final print with the picture. The result is a "married print." The sound and picture are on the same material and suitable for projection on a conventional projector.

This process is standard for all 16mm and 35mm sound films. For Super-8, this process is occasionally used, but there are variations on this procedure which are simpler and less expensive. Common Super-8 double system recording procedures which result in a "married print" are:

1. *For lip sync sound*:
   (A) Original recording is made on ¼-inch tape or cassette.

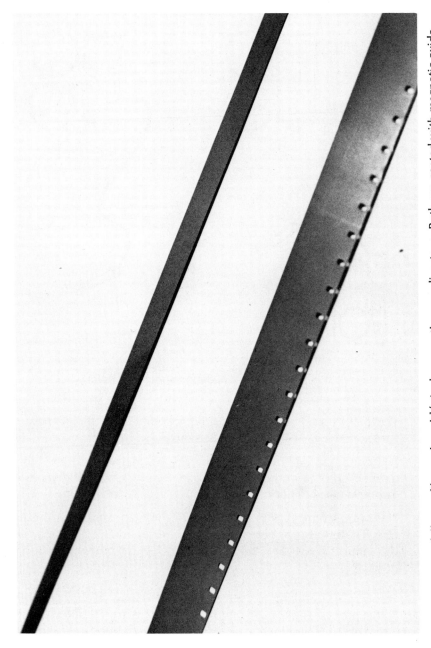

16mm magnetic full coat filmstock and ¼-inch magnetic recording tape. Both are coated with magnetic oxide for sound recording.

16mm optical soundtrack used for the making of married sound prints with conformed camera originals.

(B) Original recording is dubbed onto full coat Super-8 magnetic sprocketed film.

(C) The final print is printed onto magnetic striped film and the sound on the magnetic Super-8 full coat film is dubbed onto the magnetic stripe of the final print.

2. *For lip sync or non-lip sync films:*
   (A) Original recording is made on Super-8 magnetic full coat sprocketed film.

   (B) The final print is printed on magnetic striped film and the original recording is dubbed onto the magnetic stripe.

3. *For non-lip sync films:*
   (A) Original recording is made on ¼-inch tape or cassette.

   (B) Final print is printed on magnetic striped film and the original recording is dubbed onto the magnetic stripe.

The two processes that involve the use of Super-8 magnetic full coat stock require very specialized equipment. Working with full coat magnetic film requires the availability of a full coat recorder-playback machine, a synchronizer, and a sound reader-amplifier for editing purposes. For all three processes, a Super-8 magnetic sound projector is necessary. With this projector, one records the original sound track (from ¼-inch tape, cassette, or Super-8 full coat magnetic film) onto the magnetic stripe of the final printed film. Of course, the same projector would be needed to show the film.

All three of these processes involve procedures which are aimed at getting the film to the point where the sound and picture are combined on the same material—a final "married" print. However, the equipment to do this may not be available. Many school systems and independent filmmakers do not have magnetic sound projectors or synchronizers or Super-8 full coat recorder-reproducers. Therefore, what will follow in this chapter is a discussion of the most common and inexpensive ways of recording and reproducing sound for the beginning Super-8 filmmaker.

The procedures which will be discussed are based on double system recording and double system projection/playback. This is when a camera is used for filming and a cassette or ¼-inch recorder for recording the sound. Then, when showing the sound film, the images are projected on a conventional Super-8 projector and the sound is reproduced on a cassette or ¼-inch playback deck. With this method, lip sync sound and sync sound effects are not possible. A double system playback, involving a conventional Super-8 projector and cassette or ¼-inch recorder, simply will not hold "sync." The two machines will not run at consistent and exact speeds or hold sync for dialogue and effects. A great many people have tried to do lip sync films in this way, but with little or no success.

Types of Film Sound

Selecting the proper sound for a film can be just as creative and challenging as the shooting and editing of the film. Orson Welles has made a companion art of using sound with film and has worked just as hard at preparing and editing his sound tracks as he has in creating visual images for his films. There are a variety of types of sound which can be used with films. These are lip sync (dialogue), music, sound effects, presence (or atmosphere), and voice-over (narration, dialogue or interviews). We have already established that lip sync and sync sound effects are impossible assuming a double projection system as described above. Therefore, this discussion will be limited to non-sync sound effects, presence, music and voice-over.

Non-sync sound effects. Sound effects, in general, serve to create a sense of reality in films. The *crash* of two cars colliding, the *thud* and *splat* of a watermelon being dropped, and the *zing* of a gunshot, all make films more real and natural. The effects just mentioned are sync effects; the sound is heard as the visuals are seen. Non-sync effects are effects which occur from sounds off-screen. The *wail* of a police siren in the distance, a dog *barking* off-screen, or a phone *ringing* in an off-screen room, are all examples of non-sync effects.

Non-sync effects are used like sync effects—to create a feeling of realism and naturalism in films. In fact, off-screen effects can suggest actions and events without these actions and events actually appearing on the screen. Thus, the visual image can convey certain information while the sound track conveys extra, different information. For example:


```
INT. LIVINGROOM

1. MS JOHN SITTING IN A LIVINGROOM, READING A BOOK

   JOHN is seated in his favorite chair, reading a book.
   OFF-SCREEN SOUND EFFECT of baby crying. JOHN rises and
   exits frame left.
```

Or:

```
EXT. STREET

1. MS MARY CHANGING A FLAT TIRE

   MARY is changing a flat tire on her car. As she is doing this,
   OFF-SCREEN SOUND EFFECT of factory whistle.

2. FRONT OF FACTORY AS WORKERS EXIT
```

Both off-screen effects conveyed secondary action and both supplied an impetus for on-screen action. In the first example, John gets up and exits the frame, presumably to tend to the baby. In the second example, the factory whistle foreshadows the transition to the workers. In both examples, the sound effects were non-sync. That is, they did not literally sync up with on-screen action. But the occurrence of both on the sound track must be timed reasonably accurately. The crying baby must be timed to precede John's reaction and the factory whistle must be timed to precede the cut to the factory. With careful preparation and editing of the cassette or ¼ inch sound tracks, this kind of timing is possible for non-sync effects.

Music. Music conventionally provides a mood for a film. To put it more precisely, music complements the mood suggested by the visuals. The choice of music is very important. The music should complement and enhance the mood, tempo, and pace of the visual images in the film. There is always a temptation to come up with a visual idea based on a piece of music. This means that the visuals are generated by the music. Generally, this approach will be unsuccessful, particularly when using popular music. The central problem here is that when the visuals are a literal translation of the words or mood of a song (i.e. the visuals arise out of the song lyrics), the result is usually a low information sound film. Ideally, the sound and visuals should work together, but at the same time provide different types of information, as with the examples for sound effects discussed earlier. Music can and should work the same way. The visuals provide the action and the music provides a mood and pace for that action. When using visual accompaniment to music, the two will tend to provide the same information, which is usually amateurish and simplistic filmmaking.

Furthermore, the use of popular music, a current favorite for example, presents additional problems. The music will date very quickly. The result might be a fresh film with last year's popular favorite, which is now out of date for what the film is trying to say.

Another consideration in choosing music is a legal one. If the film is going to have some kind of commercial distribution, one cannot simply take any record or tape and use it as a sound track. Legally, this is violating the rights of the composer, the performer, and the producer who recorded that music. This legal factor is usually overlooked in the case of student films, and performers and music companies do not bring lawsuits against student films as long as the films are not put into commercial distribution. However, there have been several student and amateur films which became quite popular and received attention, but had to have their commercial progress cut short because of failure to obtain legal permission to use music.

Mixing two or more different pieces of music in the same film can present difficulties. The use of music here will be most effective if the two or more pieces of music are thematically similar but different in tempo, to match and complement the visuals they accompany. Certain cuts in the film can be "synced" to correspond to shifts in tempo and rhythm in the pieces of music, and this can be very effective. This requires careful timing and editing.

Presence and atmosphere. The presence track is a kind of sound effect and is used simply to suggest a natural sound of a particular location. For example, a feeling of realism and naturalism can be given to a film if presence tracks are used to complement visuals of a city street, countryside, or supermarket. For each visual on the screen there is a corresponding presence on the sound track.

Voice-overs. Voice-overs are a voice or voices which are used over visuals. A voice-over can be a narrator, a portion of an interview, a character voice-over, or a conversation between two or more people. Narrators are usually used in documentaries and are occasionally used for introductions to fiction films. In contemporary cinema, there is a move away from using narration, both in documentary and in fictional films. This is because narration, at its worst, is didactic. It tells the viewer what he or she is seeing. A great many contemporary documentaries avoid using narration and instead go with natural sound, dialogue, and interview voice-overs. This is another way of increasing information in the film; the visuals present one type of information and the sound track presents another. When a narrator is used to explain the visual images, these two levels of information do not exist. Therefore, a general principle is to use narration sparingly. It will work best for occasional clarification and introduction. It is weakest when it simply explains or comments on the visuals.

Interviews are often more effective and involving than narration. The use of an interview on the sound track suggests a greater degree of integration between sound and visuals than the use of a narrator does. The narrator is external to the action, an explainer and commentator. An interview, if used correctly, is logically connected to and generated by the visuals. Thus, in doing a documentary on a tattoo artist, the sound track might consist of a voice-over interview with the tattoo artist, along with interviews with people who have been tattooed. A problem to be avoided here is using interviews like narration. That is, creating a low information situation by having the content of the interview correspond directly to the visuals. The two can occasionally overlap, especially at points where the visuals need reinforcement and clarification. But in general, the two should provide different levels of information.

Character voice-over means using the voice of one or more of the characters who appear in the film on the sound track. Character voice-overs can be used to comment on the visuals and to clarify them, or they can be used to suggest memories, thoughts, or opinions of a character in the film. As with narration and interviews, character voice-overs are weakest when they provide nothing more than simple explanation. An interesting use of the character voice-over would be to experiment with first person credibility. This means to experiment with contradictions between what a character says in a voice-over and what he or she does in the visuals. There is an immediate assumption of truth when a character is presented on-screen and his or her voice-over is heard on the sound track. This assumption can be manipulated through the use of contradictions. In the opening of "Singing in the Rain", for example, Gene Kelly glamorizes his career in a "voice-over" narration, but the images shown at the same time indicate that his rise was unglamorous and comic.

Dialogue voice-overs involving the use of two or more people imply conversations relative to the action. As with all other voice-over sound, conversations as voice-overs can be used more effectively if they provide a different level of information than the visuals. For example, a scene in a film includes visuals of a couple going on a picnic. The conversation on the sound track might be a man and a woman discussing the picnic as if it were a past or future event. Therefore, the voice-over sound track could indicate their remembrances or their anticipations of the picnic, both of which could embellish the visuals.

One approach to be avoided in using character voice-overs is to attempt to fake lip sync sound. This is an approach which is usually characterized by people turning their backs to the camera to talk, people shot from the side or backwards speaking on the phone, or people holding their hands over their mouths while they speak. The point here is that in trying to fake sync sound, no one will be fooled. All the fake devices will eventually become painfully obvious. Often characters are forced to do ridiculous gestures and actions to maintain the ruse. The results of this approach are inevitably obvious and disastrous.

This discussion of the types of film sound has focused mainly on the conventional ways in which sound is used in films. It is important that these conventions for the use of sound be understood; but it is equally important to be imaginative and experiment with sound in films. Sound effects need not be used simply to create realism. A structured and systematic use of sound effects can create a kind of musical track. A certain type of music may serve as sound effects rather than as a kind of mood accompaniment. Therefore, observe how other filmmakers use sound, think of new and interesting uses for sound and experiment with different types of sound in your own films.

Techniques of Sound Recording

Both sound recording and sound reproduction work on the principles of systems and components. That is to say, recording and reproduction are based on various components doing various jobs. For recording, the components are the microphone, the recording device, and the recording medium. The microphone converts acoustical energy (sound) into electrical energy. This electrical energy travels through the microphone cable and into the recorder. The recorder pre-amplifies or processes this electrical energy and codes it onto the recording medium. In most cases, the recording medium will be ¼-inch tape or cassette audio tape. Therefore, in this process, acoustical energy is converted into electrical energy (Fig. 4-2), processed and coded, and applied to the medium by way of magnetic impulses.

The reproduction or playback components are the reproduction medium (again, ¼-inch tape or cassette tape), the reproducer (playback tape recorder), the power amplifier, and the speaker. The reproduction medium contains coded sound information. This is decoded by the playback machine and sent as electrical energy to the power amplifier. The power amplifier boosts or amplifies the intensity of the electrical signal and sends it to the speaker. The speaker performs the opposite function to the micro-

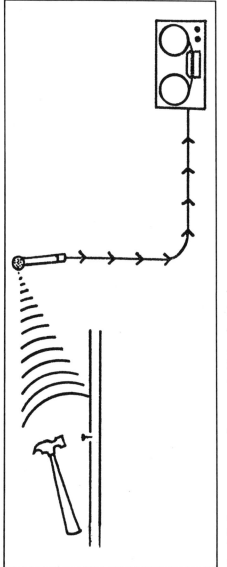

Fig. 4-2. Acoustic energy is converted into electrical energy.

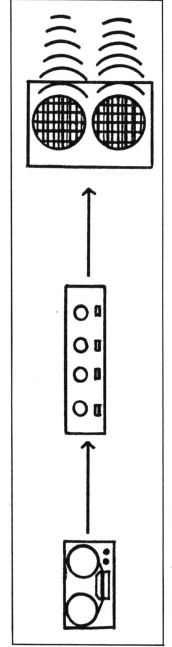

Fig. 4-3. Sound components.

phone (Fig. 4-3). It takes the electrical signal from the amplifier and converts it into acoustical energy (sound).

Any sound recording or reproducing system is only as good as every component in it. Thus, an excellent tape recorder cannot record high fidelity sound if an inexpensive, low quality microphone is used with it. Thus the most effective systems to use are those which have balanced components in terms of quality.

The foremost consideration in any recording situation is microphone placement. Microphone placement in relation to the sound source has a direct bearing on sound quality. The closer the microphone is to the source, the stronger and purer the sound signal will be. The farther the microphone is from the source, the weaker the signal. Distant microphone placement results in weak source signals and increased background noise. Optimum microphone distances can vary according to the source. In general, optimum microphone distances are:

1. For human voices (narrator, character voice-over, interview)—6 inches–18 inches.

2. For sound effects, depending on the sound intensity desired—12 inches–36 inches.

3. For presence, again depending on sound intensity desired, microphone placement should average the presence rather than pick up specifics. This placement can only be determined by testing.

Avoid placing the microphone too close to a person's mouth. If the microphone is too close, there will sometimes be "popping" and "hissing" as the person speaks sibilant letters. Inherent in all microphone placements is the notion of sound perspective. Perspective implies distance in terms of sound. An off-screen police siren usually sounds as if it is coming from a distance. This can be accomplished by using a distant microphone placement to record the siren. If the siren is recorded from a close placement and used in the film as if it were supposed to be coming from a great distance, the perspective of the sound will be wrong. This will make the sound effect less believable and less effective.

The selection of a tape recorder is important. Often there will be no choice. Only certain equipment will be available. However, if there is a choice, it will most likely be between a ¼-inch tape recorder and a cassette recorder. These two recording machines have their advantages and disadvantages. Generally speaking, a ¼-inch recorder will record and reproduce sound better than a cassette recorder. This is assuming that both are of comparable quality. The reason for this is that most ¼-inch tape recorders have variable tape speeds (1⅞" per second, 3¾" per second or 7½" per second), while all cassette recorders run only at 1⅞" per second. A faster tape speed means better sound; more tape area is used to record a sound when the recorder is running at 7½" per second than when it is running at 3¾" per second or 1⅞" per second. Therefore, when using a ¼-inch recorder, it is recommended to choose the fastest transport speed possible on the recorder. This means that more tape will be used for a given recording, but the increased sound quality is usually well worth the extra tape.

Cassette recorders are very convenient because of their portability. They are excellent for recording presence tracks, location interviews, and some location sound effects. However, the cassette recorder will usually render poor sound quality when used for music and controlled voice-overs (meaning scripted voice-overs, narration, and dialogue). In summary, use a ¼-inch recorder wherever possible. This usually means where an AC outlet is available. Use a cassette recorder for location sound work. Another great advantage of ¼-inch recorders over cassette recorders is in tape editing. Editing on a ¼-inch machine is quite easy, whereas on a cassette recorder, editing is virtually impossible. Furthermore, editing tape that has been recorded at 7½" per second is much easier than editing tape recorded at 1⅞" per second. There is a much greater distance between

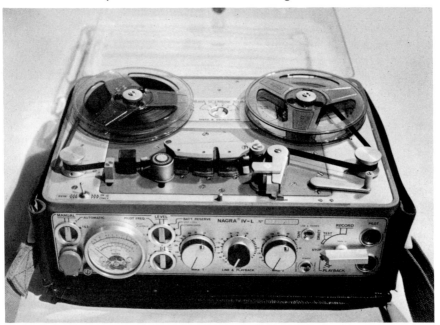

Nagra IV ¼-inch tape recorder. A professional film sound recorder.

words and sounds on tape recorded at 7½" per second and therefore more editing leeway and space.

Tape editing is a relatively simple procedure. The tools needed are the splicing block, a single edged razor blade, ¼-inch splicing tape, a grease pencil for marking, and a tape playback deck. The spot on the tape where the edit is to take place is marked with the grease pencil. Then the tape is inserted into the splicing block. The tape is cut with the razor blade diagonally (never use straight cuts) and the splice to the next sound is completed by sealing splicing tape at the junction.

Tape splicing can be used for a variety of reasons. Long interviews can be shortened and made cohesive by editing. The film can be accurately timed and non-sync sound effects can be cut in where they are desired. Music can be shortened or lengthened to coincide with the length of a film, although this practice is usually quite difficult; unless the music has a chorus or refrain which can be cut out or repeated on exact beats, the splice will usually be noticeable.

Sound Mixing

Sound mixing, or the combining of two or more sounds on a sound track, can be a very effective and efficient way of using sound for a film. Specialized sound recording equipment is needed to execute a sound mix. A sound mix can be accomplished on any stereo recorder or with two tape recorders and a sound mixer. In using the stereo recorder, one sound track is recorded on one stereo channel of the recorder and a second sound track on the other channel. This will mean, of course, that a stereo or two channel recorder will be needed to play back the mixed sound track. Thus, a sound mix might consist of a piece of music on channel A and a voice-over on channel B. The two tracks should be mixed so that the music is "under" the voice-over. That is, the voice-over should be clear and audible and the music should be audible but at a considerably lower level than the voice. These two tracks can be recorded simultaneously, but it is often easier to record them separately. On the first pass through the stereo recorder, record the voice-over. Then backwind the tape and record the music track on the opposite track.

In discussing sound recording and mixing, there are two terms which can often become confusing. These are the terms *tracks* and *channels*. Quite simply the term tracks refers to the pattern or manner in which sound is *recorded* on magnetic tape. *Channels* refers to the manner in which sound is *reproduced* off of tape. The simplest form of sound recording/reproduction is full track recording/single channel playback. This means that the full width of the recording material ¼-inch or cassette, etc.) is used to record a single sound and that this same full width is also used for playback. When speaking of stereo or four-track recording/reproduction, things get more complicated. A conventional home-use stereo ¼ inch tape recorder is usually a four-track/two-channel recorder. Sound signals are recorded on four separate tracks of the ¼-inch tape, but this kind of tape recorder can only play back two channels (stereo) in one direction. If the tape is removed from the recorder and played in the opposite direction it can also reproduce stereo sound. A four-track/four-channel recorder is considerably more versatile for recording and reproduction. The four-track/four-channel recorder records four separate sound signals on four separate tracks of the tape and can play back four separate channels for direct listening (quad sound) or for mixing purposes. This type of recorder can be used to assemble a variety of tracks (voice-over, music, sync effects, etc.) onto one material, and then these effects can be mixed down (with all levels balanced) onto full track ¼-inch or cassette for screening purposes.

When using two tape recorders and a mixer, the mix must be done simultaneously. For a voice-over and music mix with this configuration, the music off of one tape recorder is patched into the mixer and a live microphone for the voice-over is also patched into the mixer. The mixer should then be patched into the second tape deck. The mix can be balanced by the mixer into the second tape deck.

This is a very basic introduction to sound recording and mixing techniques. It is always advisable to thoroughly read and understand the manual for a piece of sound recording equipment before attempting to do a recording or mix with that piece of equipment.

Titles

It is usually during the post-production stage that the titles are prepared. There is a good reason for this. In most instances, it is not until this stage that all the credits for the production are finalized. For example, a film may be conceptualized with a certain piece of music in mind. Then, during production, a new piece of music is selected. If the music credit were shot according to the initial conception, it would have to be re-shot on the basis of the new selection. Therefore, shooting and cutting in titles should be one of the final steps in the completion of a film. The exception to this practice would be if the titles are integrated into the action of a film in the form of writing on a wall, sidewalk, etc.

There are a variety of ways in which printed titles can be presented in the film. As is discussed later, in the section on special effects, there are techniques which can be used in Super-8 filmmaking to achieve super-imposed titles. The scope of this section, however, will be limited to the preparation and shooting of printed card titles.

The title cards themselves consist of a card with the title letters attached in some way to the card. The card itself should be approximately 8 x 10 inches in size. This size corresponds quite well to the aspect ratio of the film frame. The letters should be between ½ inch and 1 inch in height. White or yellow letters on a matte black card will be more readable and pleasing to watch on film, than black letters on a white card. When white on black is filmed and projected, the letters and words are visible on the screen because the projector light is showing them onto the screen. The projector light is blocked out by the black (which is the emulsion on the film) which surrounds the letters and the result is a high contrast, easily readable title. Black on white titles, when filmed and projected, work in an opposite fashion. The projector light shows through most of the image and is resisted by the letters. This image is a little more difficult to read. Also, a major problem with this approach is that when the film becomes scratched or dirty with age, the black on white titles become very scratchy and dirty when projected and therefore, displeasing to watch. When using white letters on a black card, a transfer type, such as *Letraset* or *Presstype* will render the best results. This type is applied to the matte black card. It takes some practice to become proficient at transferring and spacing these letters. Practice, in the form of making trial words, is recommended before actually preparing the title cards.

The spacing and composition of a title is very important. Any errors in spacing and composition on the title card will be magnified many times when the title is actually projected onto the screen. Therefore, when laying down the type and composing the words of a title, be very careful about even spacing and proper alignment of words and lines of words. Always compose the titles for the rectangular film frame. There are several types of composition for titles with two or more lines. These are centered, flush left, and flush right (Fig. 4-4).

When one of these compositions is chosen, it should be consistently used. That is, all the title cards should be either flush left, centered, or flush right for a particular film. Composing the title card while shooting it is also very important. Centered titles should be composed in the middle of the frame. If the camera has a zoom lens on it, the zoom can be an aid in composing the titles. Frame the title card, then zoom in so that the title fills the frame. The left and right edges of the title should be touching the right and left edges of the frame. This will center the title horizontally and when the lens is zoomed out for the proper framing of the title, it will remain properly framed. For vertical centering, the zoom can again be used. Here the top or the bottom of the frame line is aligned with a line

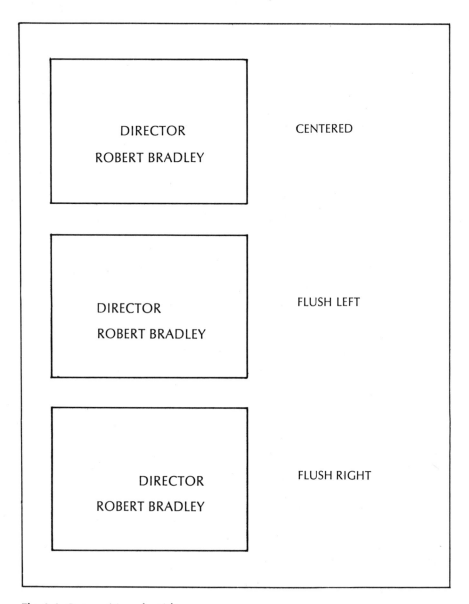

Fig. 4-4. Compositions for titles.

of words. When the lens is zoomed out for proper framing, the title will be centered vertically.

It is easiest to shoot titles on an animation stand, but in all likelihood, one will not be available. The following camera lighting configuration for shooting titles is recommended: Secure the title card to a wall. Place the camera on a tripod on the same horizontal plane as the title card and at a 90 degree angle to the title. Place one light on either side of the camera. Each light should be at approximately a 45 degree angle to the title card. Frame and compose the title card using the pan, tilt, and zoom controls.

To achieve the proper exposure for the title card, the meter system in the camera must be overridden. The internal metering system in the camera will arrive at an exposure based on the average of the scene it is reading. Therefore, it will tend to average out the main portion of the title card and will render the black portion of the card as middle grey in the exposed and processed footage. The metering system must be over-ridden so that the black portions of the title are rendered black in the processed footage. This can be accomplished by underexposing 1½ to 2 f-stops or by taking exposure off of an (18 percent grey card. Thus, if the meter reads 5.6 for a given title card, the f-stop should be overridden and re-set to f 8/11 or f 11.

Color titles when using a color film can be very effective. The colors used in the titles often correspond to a predominant color tone in the film. Thus if the film has a great many red tones in it, consider using a red title background with white letters. In this case, one can also use black letters. The problems discussed earlier in using black letters do not apply on a color background.

The time that a title is presented on screen is very important. A title that is on screen for too short or too long a time can be distracting and irritating. As a general principle, observe the following:

1. *A simple title* (the title of the film)—2–3 seconds with a 1 second fade in and one second fade out, if the camera has fade in and fade out capabilities.

2. *A credit* (for example, a film by . . .)—3 seconds with 1 second fade in and one second fade out.

3. *A double credit* (for example, camera by . . . lighting by . . .)—4–5 seconds with fade ins and fade outs.

4. *A list of credits* (for example, actors—Tom . . . Mary . . . John . . .) —3 seconds for the first line and 1–2 seconds for each additional line.

5. *A phrase or descriptive paragraph*—the reading time for the paragraph plus 50 percent. Thus, if the reading time is 10 seconds, the title should be on screen for 15 seconds.

It is always advisable to shoot more footage of each title than will actually be used in the film. This will provide leeway when editing titles into the film.

5 Special Topics

Special Effects

This section on special effects has two parts. The first deals with theory and application of special effects, or where, when, and why to use them. The second part is a breakdown of many special effects possible in Super-8 filmmaking and how they can be achieved technically.

When thinking of a special effect for a film, some basic questions should be asked: What will the effect mean to the shot or scene in which it takes place? How does it contribute to what the film is trying to do or say? Will the special effect draw attention to itself at the expense of what is happening in the film? The essence of all this is that special effects require understanding and thought. They are often over-used and abused. A film that resorts to technical gimmickry in lieu of content is often a technical exercise and nothing more. Special effects, therefore, do not exist in and for themselves. They are devices by which the filmmaker can better tell a story, make a scene or shot more effective, and draw the audience's attention where it is wanted.

Special effects should and must be integrated into the film as a whole. Their application, then, depends on an understanding of what the special effect means or does and how this relates to the point of the film in which it is used. For example, a widely used and abused effect is the soft focus to re-focus transition. This is a transition whereby at the end of one shot the image goes out of focus (by racking the lens out of focus) and the next shot begins out of focus and pulls into crisp focus. This effect is used a great deal in Super-8 filmmaking because of the difficulty in doing dissolves. This very basic special effect is based on a convention established through the years in feature fiction films. Conventionally, it was used to indicate a flashback in time. For example:

```
        INT. BATHROOM

    1.  CU JOHN LOOKING IN A MIRROR

        JOHN looks at himself in a mirror. The image GOES OUT OF FOCUS.
        As the image blurs out of focus...

        EXT. YARD

    2.  MS JOHN AS A SMALL CHILD PLAYING

        Image begins OUT OF FOCUS and PULLS INTO FOCUS, as JOHN, 5-years
        old, is playing on a swing.
```

Here, the soft focus transition is used to indicate a flashback in time and the flashback is a memory flashback. The effect is a type of film language or grammar used to indicate an element of time. However, as film has developed, film grammar has evolved. Today, it is commonplace to see:

```
        INT. BATHROOM

    1.  JOHN LOOKING IN A MIRROR

        EXT. YARD

    2.  MS JOHN AS A SMALL CHILD, PLAYING ON A SWING
```

The effect is not included, but the straight cut provides the same information. A flashback in time will be clearly understood by the audience. The point here is that film grammar has evolved as audience sophistication has developed. In the early history of the cinema, it was felt that the audience needed the special effect to understand what was happening, to remain oriented in terms of time and space presented in the film. Hence, a whole "dictionary" of film grammar was established to maintain audience orientation. This dictionary goes something like this:

Straight cut: no change in time, perhaps a change in space.

Dissolve: a passage of time indicated or a change in space.

Fade out, Fade in: a longer passage of time than a dissolve; if a change of space occurs, then a passage of time is also indicated.

Out of focus—in focus or *Ripple dissolve*: a memory flashback:

Wipe: a change in time or space or both.

Montage (e.g., spinning headlines, pages of a calendar tearing off): a passage of time.

These basic elements of film grammar developed as conventions for audience orientation. In modern cinema, with modern audience sophistication, their application is much more problematic than when they were used to create effects in the 30s and 40s. A straight cut, today, may indicate a change or no change in time or space. The films of Michelangelo Antonioni, notably *The Passenger*, use the straight cut for simple continuity, flashback, flashforward, and to represent no change in space or radical changes in space. On the other hand, the films of Bernardo Bertolucci often have dissolves which indicate no passage of time or change in space—in opposition to the established convention.

In modern-day cinema, one can say that the time and space considerations of classical film grammar conventions do not apply. In fact, many of the traditional devices have become hackneyed and have virtually disappeared, except on television. These include the ripple dissolve, the out of focus—in focus transition, and the wipe. This is true, in part, because the devices are quite obvious and heavy handed.

Dissolves and fade in—fade outs are still used frequently and quite conventionally. They can be an aid in indicating passages of time if they are used consistently and systematically. For example, one can establish different changes in time through the use of the dissolve and the fade in—fade out. The dissolve can be used to indicate a short passage of time, perhaps several hours or a portion of a day. The fade in—fade out can be used to indicate longer passages of time—a day or several days. This, of course, is relative to the time frame with which the film deals; each could represent a longer or shorter time change. The important point here is that they should be used consistently. If they are used inconsistently, their meaning, or what they indicate spatially and temporally, will become muddled.

The position presented here regarding these simple effects applies to all special effects, whether they grow out of conventions or not. The following section includes a breakdown of the most common special effects. The discussion of each special effect includes how to achieve it technically and what the effect conveys or connotes in film. Most professional special effects are done in a laboratory. A strip or strips of film are run through an optical printer and the printer creates the effect. In this way, there is a great deal of control in the execution of the effect. The discussion which follows deals with in-camera special effects—special effects which are created while running original film through the camera. Effects done in camera are usually less successful than laboratory effects, as there is less control. However, laboratory special effects can be very expensive. In-camera effects cost no more than the film stock and processing for the special effect footage.

Dissolve. As discussed earlier, a dissolve usually indicates a change in time and/or space. It is often difficult to execute a successful in-camera dissolve. The procedure is as follows: at the end of one shot, do a fade out. This can be accomplished if the camera has a shutter control lever or, if the camera has a manual exposure override, the f-stop can be used to do the fade. This will only work if the initial f-stop setting is quite low (2, 2.8 or 4), so as to have four or five f-stops for the fade. The film must now be backwound in the camera the exact number of frames equivalent to the fade out. Now the next shot is set up and begun with a fade in which should be the same length as the previous fade out and backwinding. This procedure will create on film a fade out and fade in with an overlap or a dissolve. Several brands of Super-8 cameras have backwinding features to create dissolves and superimpositions. However, this is mechanically difficult because most Super-8 film is sealed inside the Super-8 cartridge. Some 16mm cameras, notably the spring wound Bolex models, have backwind and variable shutter control mechanisms. Even with a very versatile camera, in-camera dissolves are often difficult to achieve. Both takes of both shots must work. Both fades must be reasonably accurate and backwinding must be precise.

Fade out—Fade in. The fade out to fade in convention indicates some passage of time, more than a dissolve, and/or a change in space. On cameras with a variable shutter, these are very easily executed. If the camera has no variable shutter, the f-stop override control can be used as discussed above. When working in an interior, the lights can be used to create the fade. When using lights for fading, all the lights must be turned off or on simultaneously. The exposure must be overridden and locked to the shooting f-stop number; otherwise, the in-camera meter will try to compensate during the change in light. There is a commercial product on the market known as Foto-fade. This is a black, paint-like substance which the film is dipped into and dyed to create a fade. Good results can occasionally be achieved with Foto-fade but it is messy to work with.

Mattes. Mattes are forms which can be simply attached to the front of the lens. These are hard to work with as the position of the matte will change as the lens is focused. Matte shots are best achieved with the use of a matte box. These can be homemade (Fig. 5-1). The use of the matte often suggests a subjective shot. For example, a keyhole shot or binocular matte indicates what someone is seeing.

An Arriflex 16S with matte box.

Wipes. The only kind of in-camera wipes which are possible are wipes to or from black. The conventional scene-to-scene wipe, where one shot is wiped off the screen by another, can only be accomplished by a sophisticated optical printing process. Simple wipes to or from black usually indicate change in time and/or space, much like a fade in—fade out. They can be quite interesting if the direction of the wipe relates to some movement or action in the film. For example, a scene of someone running from left to right could be started with a wipe from black which goes from left to right. Or, for experimentation or humor, a wipe might be used to push a character off the screen. Mechanically, the wipe is simply accomplished by putting a black card over the lens and pulling it out of the way, either

Fig. 5-1. A homemade matte box.

left to right, bottom to top or diagonally. For better control, the matte box device can be used. The matte box can hold the wipe card steady and help make the wipes themselves smoother.

Superimpositions. Superimpositions are only possible if the camera has backwind capability. As discussed earlier, most Super-8 cameras have a very limited backwind capability, if they have it at all. The super or double exposure takes place when two shots appear simultaneously on the screen on top of one another. This is accomplished by filming one shot, backwinding the camera and then filming a different shot. To avoid overexposure, it is recommended that each shot be underexposed by one half to one full f-stop.

A super suggests the blending of two spaces or time frames. It is conventionally used for dreams or memories to bring two different spaces or time frames together.

Superimposed titles. Titles that appear over a scene are superimposed titles or burn-through titles. Like supered scenes, these can only be accomplished in the camera if it has a backwind feature. The procedure is that the scene over which the titles are to be supered is shot first. Then the camera is backwound to the start of the shot and the titles are filmed. Only white or yellow titles which are placed or written on a matte black surface or card will burn through. A type of superimposed title can be done with the use of a mirror. The titles are fixed to the mirror. The mirror is angled to reflect the desired shot and the titles are filmed by the camera. A large mirror, mounted on a frame, will work best. The focusing for this shot can present problems. The focus setting for the titles is the distance from the camera to the mirror. The focus setting for the scene reflecting off of the mirror is the distance from the camera to the mirror plus the distance from the mirror to the actual elements of the scene (Fig. 5-2). Therefore, depth of field must be sufficiently great if it is to include both focus ranges. Applying the rules and factors that affect depth of field, the following is recommended for this shot:

1. Use a large mirror, perhaps 2' x 4'.

2. Have the mirror mounted securely (in a frame device).

3. Have the mirror at least 4–6 feet from the camera.

4. Try to shoot at an f-stop above 5.6.

5. Use as wide an angle lens as possible to improve depth of field.

6. Have the subject being reflected in the mirror as close as possible to the mirror.

7. Be sure not to include signs or moving cars in the scene; remember, the reflected image will be a "mirror" image.

Other mirror shots. Some very interesting shots and effects can be accomplished with the use of a large mirror. For example, filming a character in front of a mirror can provide an opportunity to manipulate the background behind the character. This can be done by moving the mirror during the shot. The character will remain stationary but the background will change. This is a shot which must be very carefully set up and rehearsed, but when executed properly, the results can be very pleasing.

A mirror can also be used to create a wipe. For this, a scene is filmed off of a mirror, and during the shot the mirror is pulled out of the way, revealing the scene behind the mirror. A mirror with straight edges and no border is a must here, as the object is to disguise the fact that the first part of the shot is a mirror reflection. If moving the mirror is too difficult, the camera can be panned away from the mirror to reveal the scene behind it. A mirror can also be used for a split screen effect. Here, a mirror with straight edges and no border is positioned half-way into the frame. The mirror will reflect what is in front of it and this will be half the image in the frame. The other half of the image will be made up of what is next to the mirror.

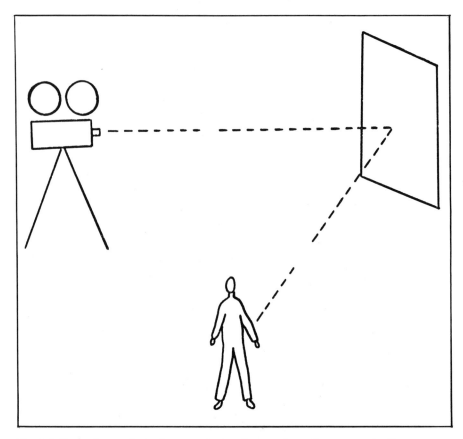

Fig. 5-2. Focus for a mirror shot equals the distance from the camera to the mirror plus the distance from the mirror to the subject.

Shooting with the camera upside down. A variety of effects can be achieved by shooting with the camera upside down and projecting the resulting footage tails first. The projected footage will show everything going backwards (reverse motion). If this footage is projected normally, heads first, the image will be simply up-side down on the screen. But if the tail of the film is projected, the image will be right-side up, but moving in reverse. This effect is usually done for comedy, but variations on it can be used for a variety of special effects.

If this technique is used and a character walks backwards down a city street, the projected footage will show the character walking forwards down the street, while everyone else is moving backwards. Employing this technique to film a character walking backwards and throwing a hat from her head to the ground will, when projected, show the character walking forward with the hat flying off the ground and onto her head.

This technique can be used effectively for "swish" pans. A swish pan is a very fast type of pan that stops precisely on a predetermined framing. If the film is shot normally, this is very difficult; the pan must stop precisely on the desired framing. If the up-side down camera technique is used, the swish pan can be executed very precisely. The shot should start on the desired framing, which is to follow the pan when projected. Then the camera should pan quickly away from this framing. The projected footage will have the swish pan with the precise stop on the desired framing. Swish pans are generally used for spatial transitions and, if used systematically and consistently, can be effective.

Refilming techniques. By refilming a projected image off a screen, a variety of effects can be achieved. The basic set-up for refilming is (Fig. 5-3):

1. Put the projector very close to the screen to get a small, sharp image.

2. Place the camera on a tripod very close to the projector.

3. Use a fast film (like Tri-X or Ektachrome 160) and let the automatic exposure system in the camera determine the proper exposure (it will usually be f-2 or 2.8 with Tri-X).

The refilmed image will always be inferior to the original. Grain and contrast will increase considerably. So although a great many effects can be done by refilming, the resulting image is always poor in quality.

If the projector has still frame capability, the refilming technique can be used to create a freeze frame. Freeze frames emphasize a particular element in time and space.

Burn-through titles can be created by using a double projector refilming set-up (Fig. 5-4). On one projector, set up the live action shot. On the second projector, thread up the titles (white or yellow letters on black). If both images are projected simultaneously, the titles will appear over the live action footage. By turning the lamp on and off on the projector which is projecting the titles, the titles can be made to fade in and fade out. This double projection set-up can also be used for two scene superimpositions.

Fig. 5-3. A simple refilming set-up.

The refilming process also makes it possible to change the motion speed of a particular shot. A normal speed shot (18 fps) can be changed to slow motion by projecting at 6 fps and refilming at 18 fps or by projecting at 18 fps and refilming at 48 fps. The latter can create problems in exposure, as the faster in-camera shutter speed means a larger f-stop opening is necessary.

Similarly, a shot can be changed to fast motion by projecting at 48 fps and refilming at 18 fps or by projecting at 18 fps and refilming at 6 fps.

Fig. 5-4. A double projection refilming set-up.

Zoom-dolly effect. A very interesting special effect can be achieved by zooming and dollying at the same time. The principle here is to maintain the camera framing on a shot by zooming in and dollying out simultaneously (or zooming out and dollying in). The result will be that the framing will remain the same but the perspective in the shot will change. Alfred Hitchcock used this shot to great effect in *Vertigo*. The shot has a disorienting effect and is often used for mystery, suspense, or horror.

To be effective, the speed of the zoom and the speed of the dolly should be perfectly synchronized and smooth so there is no perceptible change in framing. In amateur filmmaking, this can be very difficult to accomplish. Best results are obtained when using a tripod or fixed dolly rather than a hand-held dolly.

Animation, pixilation, stop-motion. There are a variety of excellent textbooks on film animation techniques, and we recommend that a film-maker wishing to produce an animated film consult one of these texts. However, the techniques of pixillation and stop motion fall into the category of special effects and will be discussed here.

Pixilation means filming a moving subject at a very slow transport speed in order to speed up the motion or action in the projected image. Thus, a city scene, when filmed at 6 fps will be moving three times as fast when projected at 18 fps. A famous pixilation film, *Neighbors* by Norman McLaren, uses pixilation techniques to emphasize and exaggerate how two neighbors fight over property lines. In pixilation, the slower the transport speed, the greater the effect of speeding up the motion in the projected image. Extremely slow transport speeds like one frame per minute or one frame per hour can be accomplished manually with a tripod and cable release (on Super-8 cameras with single frame capability) or with an intervalometer. An intervalometer is a device that can be pre-set for a desired transport speed and which will automatically single-frame the camera at the preset rate. Some expensive Super-8 cameras have built-in intervalometers. This type of pixilation is often called time-lapse cinematography and has been used to show flowers blooming, etc. There is a formula for determining the transport speed for pixilation or time-lapse cinematography (assuming a projection transport speed of 18 fps):

1. Compute the total time of the event to be filmed into seconds.

2. Determine the total number of seconds of film screen time for this event and multiply by 18.

3. Divide no. 2 into no. 1. This will be the transport speed in seconds per frame.

To illustrate, let's say that one wishes to film a sunrise. In pre-production planning and scouting it is determined that the period of time it takes the sun to rise is two hours.

2 hrs. $\times$ 60 mins. $\times$ 60 secs. = 7200 seconds.

It is also determined that in context, the sunrise should take twenty seconds of screen time.

$$20 \times 18 = 360 \text{ frames.}$$

$$360\overline{)7200} = 20.$$

So, shooting one frame every 20 seconds will convert a two-hour sunrise into a 20 second pixilated sequence of film time.

Stop Motion also entails a single framing technique. In using stop motion the filmmaker actually "animates" objects by moving them and single framing, thus creating movement on film of inanimate things, objects, etc. A great many special effects in recent science fiction films (*Star Wars*, for example) are created using stop-motion techniques. Television commercials (the *Pillsbury doughboy*, for example) often use stop-motion techniques.

Following are some suggestions for successful stop-motion cinematography:

1. For a single stop-motion scene the camera must be firmly mounted on a steady, stable tripod. Unwanted camera movement can ruin a stop motion sequence. Using a cable release is strongly suggested.

2. The movement of objects in front of the camera must be carefully planned. Moves should be based on increments so that the projected image has movement which is smooth and accurately timed.

Stop motion is often created by "double framing"; that is, two frames are shot for each increment. Double framing makes for smooth moves and saves time. Let's consider the following example:

> A stop-motion sequence is to consist of several dominos on a tabletop which are to move around the tabletop, form different patterns, climb over one another, etc. The scene will be projected at 18 fps in its finished form and a double framing technique will be used. Thus, each second of screen time will be broken into 9 increments of 2 frames each. So, if one domino is to move across the entire tabletop in 2 seconds, the distance it is to move is broken into 18 increments. The distance might be 1½ ft. (18 inches). Therefore, the domino should be moved 1 inch and the camera should then shoot 2 frames. The domino is moved another 1 inch, the camera exposes 2 frames, etc., until the sequence is complete.

.

It is obvious that stop-motion techniques require a great deal of time and planning to execute successfully. However, the results are often pleasing and entertaining.

Throughout this chapter, we have outlined many in-camera special effects. Not all possible special effects have been covered. There are a great many more special effects possible with the use of a matte box, re-filming techniques, and mirror techniques than were mentioned above. Of course, any special effect should be considered in light of the esthetic principles outlined at the beginning of this section. Again, we emphasize that virtually all in-camera special effects will never be as successful as special effects created in the lab. The film generational process, described in Chapter 4, is the process which allows the greatest freedom and control for special effects. Special effects usually created in a lab or film optical house are: dissolves, fade ins and fade outs, superimpositions, burn-through titles, and freeze frames. If lab effects are to be included in a film, the film originals must be conformed for printing purposes. For lab effects, it is recommended that a lab be contacted for specific set-up procedures, and a text that deals specifically with the mechanics of film editing and conforming be consulted.

Using the Zoom

The problem of the zoom is to determine when to use it and what it actually communicates or can communicate. For the amateur (and all too often, the professional), the zoom is used simply because it is there. It is hard to resist. A primary reason for this is that the zoom is a tool which the camera operator can use to insert his or her personality onto that which he or she is shooting. It provides an added element of control. It is clearly for this reason that directors, both amateur and professional, often either prefer cameras with no zooms, or inform their camera operators that they are not to zoom unless so instructed. The answer to when to use the zoom and what it communicates and can communicate in a fiction film can be answered in part by looking at the way in which the zoom is used in the non-fiction film, primarily in news photography and documentaries. One writer has said that in both reporting and documentary, the zoom is "simply a device which allows us to get close," a device to "move into a close-up of someone being interviewed, for example, or to point out a particular detail in a football match without making a cut."

A basic disagreement with this conception of the use of the zoom lens in reporting and verité hinges on the proper use of the zoom. The use of the zoom lens in newsfilm or documentary is to permit the camera op- erator to stay with an action which he or she would not be able to follow without the zoom. This might well mean that the camera does not zoom in to get closer, but zooms out to cover a broader part of the emerging scene. A cut is not always possible in a news situation. To cut is to lose the moment. If a close-up is required in reality, it is required immediately, and the zoom is capable of that immediacy.

With that immediacy, with that need for not losing the reality of the moment, is the knowledge that some force, the cameraperson, is making decisions about what is necessary to convey the reality of the moment and what is important about that moment. Often in documentary, the camera moves, the lens zooms in to the wrong framing and re-adjusts, searching out the essentials of the situation. There is no objectivity. The reality of the situation is filtered through the cameraperson and we accept it. There is no attempt to deceive; there can be none, because we are all too aware of the camera being in someone's hands. In fact, part of our appreciation depends on the realization that what we see in newsfilm or documentary is unfolding before us as it did the first and only time for the person holding the camera.

Certainly, in such situations, movement of the zoom does not corres- pond to the movement of the cameraperson and it is acceptable to us be- cause we accept the technology which makes it possible. We do not say, as for example in *The Underwater Adventures of Jacques Cousteau,* that a zoom from across the deck of the Calypso to the face of Cousteau does not correspond to the way we see things. The technology is there and we accept it because it helps us understand the situation we see. A cut from one side of the deck to a close-up of Cousteau would have annoyed us, and made us ask what had been cut out and why we had been excluded from the decision.

Thus it is broadly accepted that the use of the zoom lens is quite ap- propriate for newsfilm and documentary, for conveying real situations. What are the implications of this acceptance of the use of the zoom lens in the fiction film, either amateur or professional? Clearly, it is appropriate to use the zoom in a fiction film if one is trying to create the illusion of documentary or news. The use of the hand-held camera and zoom in the television reporting sequence in *Night of the Living Dead* contribute strongly to the aura of horrible reality in the film. A rock-steady image from a dolly would have ruined the effect. The one time in a television news sequence in the film when a cut is employed (when the camera moves suddenly from a few feet outside the general's car in Washington to across the street), the viewer is disturbed not because of the cut, but because from the new camera position we see the car we had been next to the previous second, and we do not see the camera through which we had been looking. Time and immediacy have been violated.

Skill and artistry are debatable, but as a general rule, it seems appropriate to say that the zoom lens can be used freely when attempting to recreate an atmosphere or create an image of documentary, especially in the presentation of a quasi-news event.

A second use of the zoom stemming from news and documentary involves the use of the close-up. In a real situation, the camera can go from a medium shot to a close-up, and does so with the zoom to keep from losing any conversation or reaction and to concentrate on the individual who has become the center of interest. While the cut is accepted in the fiction film for such purposes, it is no more or less natural than a zoom. The cut is merely an accepted technique. The presence of a chooser, someone electing to make that move, is just as evident in the cut as it is in the zoom. It can even be argued that the zoom is less disruptive because it is continuous and allows the performance to continue without interruption. Neither the cut nor the zoom duplicates eye movement. The technique employed in either case should be the one appropriate to that which is being expressed and should not be prescribed by an arbitrary esthetic principle. The zoom lens is no more evil today than sound was in 1927.

Thus, principles one and two are that the zoom can be used to duplicate an atmosphere of documentary and to move into a close-up to avoid the loss of immediacy in a performance or expression. Beyond this, in the fiction film, we move into speculation and experience. It becomes a question of what has worked and why, rather like principles of common law. We are sure creative people will devise new ways to use the zoom lens, some of which will work and others of which will not. Only usage (as in grammar) will finally determine what is appropriate for the lens, not arbitrary decisions. Therefore, realizing that they are tentative, we will set forth some uses of the zoom lens which have been attempted and the limits of their use, in addition to a few possible uses of the zoom lens which may not have been fully explored.

Zooms can be used for tracking. The zoom need not be a substitute for a tracking shot, but a different way of tracking. The principles of perspective should be considered here. A zoom in "flattens" out the image, the film image is "flatter" when shot with a telephoto lens. The zooms at the beginning of François Truffaut's *Wild Child* tend to merge the child with the surrounding woods as the zoom moves back losing the child in a jigsaw of trees and leaves. For these shots, the zoom is more effective than a tracking shot.

Zooms can be used to emphasize distance. A telephoto lens can bring a figure close from a great distance, but it cannot tell us how far from the object we are. The normal lens can emphasize the distance but not bring us into contact with the object. A zoom shot, pulling back over a great distance, can do many things at once. It can emphasize the smallness of an object or person in the total landscape, emphasize the great distance between points or people and create a variety of compositions within one shot which may be striking and pleasing.

Zooms can be used for sudden dramatic emphasis. Zooms can be used for such emphasis if used sparingly. The primary use of the zoom for dramatic emphasis is to indicate the sudden revelation of a shock through the eyes of a character. Such zooms can be effective, but for them to be integrated into the film they should generally be used in character point of view seeing shots, the implication being that a character reaction is emphasized through the use of a sudden zoom.

Zooms are excellent for moving into freeze frames. Because a zoom in does flatten out the image, it is an ideal device for moving into a freeze frame, which is essentially a recreation of the feeling of a two dimensional photograph.

Zooms can be used for special effects. The primary effects for which zooms have been used to date have been to indicate hallucination, drunkenness, or another abnormal state of mind, with the lens moving in and out. We do not deny their use for such purposes. However, their effectiveness for these effects is, to date, problematic.

Zooms can be used to replace other lenses. This is a primary reason for the use of zooms by amateurs and those for whom the changing of lenses under particular situations is not possible or desirable. Simply put: just because the zoom lens can zoom during a shot is no reason why it must. Instead of having three lenses, the zoom can be set at fixed positions for shots to approximate the other lenses which might otherwise be used. In fact, it would seem to be the precise reason why Super-8 cameras will often have only a zoom lens. Of course, there is a loss of image quality when a zoom is used for the purpose of substituting for other lenses, but often the loss of quality is slight and well worth the convenience and spontaneity of the variable focal length lens. It may be hard to restrain one's desire to zoom while the camera is operating, but such restraint can often give the lens more range. As zooms improve, and the better ones appear near perfection, it is quite likely that various other lenses will not be needed.

Color and Black and White

Deciding whether a film will be in black and white or in color is one of the most important of the filmmaker's decisions, but it is often the decision to which he or she gives the least thought. The technical limitations which formerly dictated decisions about whether black and white or color were to be used are gone. However, too many filmmakers cling to clichés which are no longer valid. For example, several years ago, if one were going to make a cinema verité film—shooting an indoor basketball game, or a town meeting, or following a concert tour—one could only shoot in black and white. It was also established that the black and white Hollywood feature film was dead, because black and white films had little television sales potential. *The Elephant Man* and *Stardust Memories* may be unique, or may re-open the possibility of the black and white feature film, but this is as irrelevant to the non-professional filmmaker as is the idea that cinema verité can only be in black and white. The non-professional and the professional, to the extent that they can, should decide whether to use black and white on the basis of what they will say in their films and not on what they have heard they "should" do.

There are three major clichés about making the choice between black and white and color which have to be discarded before the filmmaker can make his or her decision.

Cliché 1: Color is more expensive than black and white.

There is no doubt that color is more expensive in 16mm, but not remarkably so. A rough rule of thumb is that color costs about 50 percent more for 16mm. But for Super-8, there is no essential difference in the cost between black and white and color.

Cliché 2: It is easier to shoot in black and white than in color.

There are problems with both. Essentially, we would argue that color is easier to shoot in most lighting situations. To do a professional job with lighting, black and white requires a great deal of thought and mastery of lighting techniques. One of the greatest problems of the non-professional filmmaker is the handling of light, particularly in black and white films. Color can be lit flatter and with greater reliance upon color and décor to carry the mood of the scene. Shooting in black and white demands careful consideration of the light areas and shadow areas in each shot, which many people find difficult or impossible to do with the naked eye. Color is easier to estimate in terms of lighting and contrast than black and white.

In conjunction with this, although color films require somewhat more light than comparable black and white films, if comparable contrast is to be obtained, it is often a matter of degree rather than of kind. Or, to put it another way, stronger lights may be needed for color, but probably fewer lights will be needed and this means a less complex set-up. In essence, the fewer the lights, the easier the shot.

Cliché 3, and perhaps the most important: Black and white is more "real" than color.

The basis for this belief, one of the most firmly established of film clichés and one which many filmmakers will defend with zeal, is found in the history of film. The idea that color represents artifice is tied to the fact that film originated and developed in black and white. It simply was not possible to have commercially usable color film when motion pictures originated in the 1890s. The world film audience grew up conditioned to black and white as being the basic "color" of film. Whatever early color was seen in films was associated with artifice. As early as 1895, audiences saw movies in Edison's Kinetoscope colored by hand. An exotic dancer shimmied while colors poorly painted on the film were intended to resemble colored lights. Ten years later, in 1905, Pathé Frères was using stencils to apply colors for fantasy films such as *Down in the Deep*, which included pink pixies underwater with green whales.

The equation of color with fantasy continued, and the supposedly artistic hand-painted colors were particularly jarring and unnatural in a wide variety of films, including Cecil B. DeMille's *Fool's Parade* (1922), which included several hand-painted scenes. But hand painting gave way to tinting, a process whereby scenes and entire films were tinted a specific color, usually one color intending to bring about a particular emotional response. Again, tinting does not coincide with our vision of intentional artifice. It may have been a very effective artifice, but the connotation was that it was creatively artificial as opposed to black and white films which were somehow natural because people were accustomed to them. Tinted sections of Rupert Julian's *Phantom of the Opera* with Lon Chaney (1925) are perfect examples of emotional tinting. In 1931, James Whale's *Frankenstein* was issued in "ghastly green." In 1966 Claude LeLouch used tinted sequences in *A Man and A Woman* to indicate "unreal" emotional images and response. Two-color tinting emerged as early as 1933, but the effect was equally artificial and essentially the same.

Actually, shooting in color was possible as early as 1909 with a process called Kinemacolor. Restricted to reds and browns using filters while the frames alternated between red and green, the process must indeed have been bizarre. Shooting in color was considered a gimmick and was a kind of pop experiment, even though the Kinemacolor process was used to shoot a seldom seen two-and-one-half-hour newsreel of the crowning of

King George V as Emperor of India. Other color processes, such as Prisma-color, did little to break down the gap between bizarre color and some approximation of how the eye sees color, or how we think it sees color. Prismacolor was used to photograph the American flag, which came out fine in two colors, but the sky behind it was grey and the grass an eerie brown.

Technicolor arose in 1917 with a feature called *The Gulf Between*. The first Technicolor was a two color process—red and blue only. Technicolor sequences were incorporated into such films as DeMille's *The Ten Com-mandments* (1925), Fred Niblo's *Ben Hur* (1925), and Eric Von Stroheim's *The Wedding March* (1926). A total of 57 features were shot in two-color Technicolor, the last and possibly the best of which was Michael Curtiz's *The Mystery of the Wax Museum* (1933). By 1932–3, three-color Techni-color arrived with Walt Disney's *Flowers and Trees* and *Three Little Pigs*, and the first feature in this process was *Becky Sharp* in 1935.

Four problems or conditions existed for the Technicolor process that caused it to be equated further in the public mind artificiality and fantasy. First, Technicolor films had low ASA's—as low as 3. Not until *Gone With the Wind* (1939) did they get up even as high as 12 or 16. To shoot this film required a tremendous amount of special artificial lighting and re-flectors, even when filming outdoors. This often became painful for the performers, affecting their performance and restricting their movements. Second, color shooting required special makeup for the actors because the quality of the technicolor process, until a few years ago, was such that natural skin tones did not appear natural. This added a further artifice because the makeup never looked quite natural. Third, the nature of the color in early three-color processes was such that it could not approxi-mate natural colors. As a matter of fact, many studios and filmmakers consciously exploited this by painting their sets strong pastel colors. The effect, as in Michael Curtiz's and William Keighley's *The Adventures of Robin Hood* (1938) could be beautiful, but did not approximate "real" color. Fourth, the expense of color—cameras, film processing, lights, makeup—made the studios use it sparingly and only for extravaganzas and costume spectacles. A film which worked within the low-key mode was never considered for color. Therefore, the costume spectacles and musicals could, through the 1940s, be counted on to be in color, while more visually naturalistic films, such as the detective films, smaller budget westerns and their like, would naturally be done in less expensive black and white.

By the late 1950s, new films and lighting had made color film less expensive and more flexible to work with. This flexibility, combined with the loss of audiences to television, made color and wide screen central to the hopes of the industry to draw people from their television sets. The genre films—detective stories, war films, etc.—dwindled and the big color spectacles increased. The equation of color and the unreal continued and expanded. When the demands of television for features in color appeared in the 1960s, all films went to color, leaving black and white to the so-called documentary filmmakers and amateurs who could not afford or handle color.

It might be argued that because of this tradition of color, there is a psychological justification for the continuance of black and white to represent a "real" mode of expression. If the argument is valid, it is at best a temporary one based on a rapidly changing history. Films date quickly. The concept of black and white to represent reality has, as a result of faster, more accurate color films, all but gone.

With this questioning of some of the basic assumptions about color and black and white, we offer a new series of guidelines for the choice of black and white and color in making non-professional films. Again, we emphasize that the selection of either mode is primarily a matter of what the film is to say rather than what the supposed technical limitations are. With this in mind, here are some tentative guidelines for choosing between black and white and color. All these guidelines may be erased in the next ten years by changing technology, and all of them are flexible. For every guideline, there is an exception.

1. It is easier to create and sustain "down" moods with black and white: terror, sadness, nostalgia, melodrama. Therefore, for strong mood films, such as horror films, low key interviews, and some social documentaries, one should seriously consider black and white.

2. By the same token, high mood films involving comedy and spectacle might well be in color to take advantage of the feeling of celebration and animation given by color, a feeling which is a result of the warmth of color in most current color films.

3. The choice should be made on the basis of the dominant motif of the film. There may be sad interludes in the film, but if the essence of the film is animated and comic, color would be the wisest choice.

4. Switching from black and white to color in a single film is seldom a good idea. The change is always jarring and raises a conscious question in the mind of the viewer about what is happening instead of letting the visual impact of the film carry itself. However, that may well be exactly what the filmmaker wants. It was, in part, what Lindsay Anderson wanted in *If . . .* and the Polish director Marek Hlesko wanted in *The Eighth Day of the Week* (in which a fantasy sequence in a department store is the only color sequence in a black and white naturalistic film).

5. If décor is particularly important to a film—if the sets are an essential part of the narrative and what the film is saying, then color film is preferable. The Hammer horror films such as *Dracula Has Risen from the Grave*, Roger Corman's horror films such as *The Mask of the Red Death*, or the films of Curtis Harrington such as *What's the Matter with Helen?* or *Who Slew Auntie Roo?*, rely heavily upon their color and décor to carry the mood of horror.

6. One of the few technical considerations to bear in mind is that if the film is to be shot both indoors and outdoors, and the indoor shooting prohibits the use of extra lights, fast black and white will render better results. As mentioned earlier, color film shot under available light yields poor images.

7. When in doubt, use color. The day of color is here. Black and white may well become a specialized mode for specialized projects. The varieties of color film stocks will soon be sufficient to handle any mood or mode.

Glossary

(see pages 43–44 for definitions of scriptwriting terms)

A & B ROLLING—The process used in preparing original footage for printing. Also called checkerboarding. A & B rolling creates invisible splices in 16mm and Super-8 and allows for laboratory effects such as dissolves, superimpositions, and burn-through titles.

ACADEMY APERTURE—The standard frame ratio for most film formats. This ratio is 4:3 or 1:1.33 in Super-8 and 16mm.

AMPLIFIER—A sound component used to increase a sound signal, usually to a speaker.

ANAMORPHIC LENS—A type of lens used to "squeeze" images on a standard gauge film. Used for wide screen processes such as CinemaScope.

ANGLE OF VIEW—The horizontal angle, measured in degrees, that a given lens accepts. For example, a normal lens accepts an angle of view of 22–23 degrees.

ANIMATION—A type of filmmaking whereby single frames are recorded individually (single frame), rather than the film running continuously through the camera. There are a variety of types of animation including cell animation, pixilation, stop motion (object animation), cut-out animation and kinestasis.

ANSWER PRINT—The first print of a film made from conformed originals.

APERTURE—This can have two meanings. It can refer to the iris f-stop opening in a lens. It can also refer to the frame ratio for a given format (see ACADEMY APERTURE).

ASA—The sensitivity of the film being used.

AVAILABLE LIGHT—The light which exists naturally in any given shooting situation, as opposed to artificial light.

BACK LIGHT—A type of light usually used behind and above a subject. The back light creates depth in the image by separating the subject from the background.

BACK PROJECTION—A studio process (also called "rear projection") whereby an image is projected onto a screen behind actors so that they appear to be at the location of the projected image. This process is usually used to save money in production; the actors remain in the studio for shooting, yet in the final film appear to be on location.

BARN DOOR—Leaf devices on a lighting unit used to control the throw of the light.

BARNEY—A cloth covering for a camera used to eliminate camera noise in a sync sound shooting situation.

BEAM SPLITTER—A prism device in a lens or viewing system which diverts some percentage of the light entering the lens to the viewing system and allows a greater percentage of the light to pass onto the film plane.

BLIMP—A soundproof hard shell enclosure for the camera, used to eliminate camera noise in sync sound shooting situations.

BLOW-UP—An optical printing process whereby one gauge is enlarged to another. For example, a Super-8 film may be blown up onto 16mm film.

BURN-IN—A type of title, usually white or yellow lettering, which is superimposed over a live action sequence.

CABLE RELEASE—A device used for single framing or for operating the camera remotely.

CHANGEOVER—The process whereby, during the projection of a film, the switch is made between one projector showing a reel of the film and the next projector which is to show the next reel of the film.

CINCH MARKS—Black scratches on film created as a result of winding a roll too tightly.

CINEMATOGRAPHER—The camera operator or cameraperson.

CLAW—The small internal arm in a camera or projector which engages in a sprocket hole and pulls a frame into position for exposure or projection.

CLAPPER BOARD—The slate which is used to identify a take in sync sound shooting. The slate creates a sound and visual reference which is used for "syncing" the sound and picture during editing.

COLOR CORRECTION—The use of color filters to make color films respond more naturally to the scene being filmed. In printing, color correction filters are used to correct color imbalance in the original footage.

COLOR TEMPERATURE—A measurement in degrees Kelvin which indicates the color "balance" of a film stock or a lighting situation. 3200K and 3400K are standard indoor color temperatures and approximately 6000K is the outdoor color temperature.

CONTRAST—The relationship between blacks and whites and greys in a scene or shot.

COVER SHOT—Also called a master shot. Recording a scene in its entirety, usually in an MS or MLS.

CUTAWAY—A cut which is away from the central action. A reaction shot is a type of cutaway.

CUT-IN—A cut which is into the central action. This is usually a magnified portion of a scene in the form of a CU.

DAILIES—Unedited workprint footage. Called dailies because in most feature film shooting situations the workprints for a day's shooting are prepared on a daily basis for screening and evaluation by cast and crew. Also called rushes.

DEEP FOCUS—A shooting technique utilizing great depth of field.

DEPTH OF FIELD—The range, in terms of distance near and distance far, that subjects or objects in a shot will be in acceptably sharp focus.

DIAPHRAGM—The f-stop iris.

DIFFUSION—Changing the characteristic of a lighting unit by making the light softer.

DIOPTER—The adjustment on most reflex cameras allows the viewing system of the camera to be adjusted to the cameraperson's vision.

DOLLY—A device, usually on wheels or castors, onto which the camera is mounted for moving camera shots.

DOUBLE EXPOSURE—Exposing a film image twice by making the film pass twice through the camera.

DOUBLE SYSTEM—A sync sound recording system in which the image is recorded in the camera and the sound is recorded on a separate recorder. Double system projection is a projection system whereby the image is projected on a projector and the sound is reproduced via an interlocked full coat playback machine, a ¼-inch player or a cassette player.

DUBBING—A post-production process in which lip sync dialogue or sync sound effects are dubbed or "synced" with an image in a recording studio.

EMULSION—The light sensitive substance coated on the film. The emulsion consists of light sensitive silver halides suspended in a gel.

EQUALIZATION—In sound recording, the filtration or "balancing" of a recording in terms of highs, lows and mid-range.

EXPOSURE—What happens when light strikes raw film stock.

EXPOSURE METER—A meter which measures the intensity of light in a scene in terms of middle grey. In amateur filmmaking the meter is often an in-camera meter. In professional filmmaking a separate hand-held meter is used for determining exposure.

F-STOP—A number which indicates the opening of the iris in the lens.

FILTERS—In shooting and printing, filters are used to correct color, change contrast, reduce light, or reduce reflections.

FILTER FACTOR—The amount of light that a filter absorbs. A filter factor of 2 equals a light reduction of one f-stop. A factor of 4 equals two f-stops, a factor of 8 equals three f-stops, etc.

FINE CUT—The first tightly-edited version of a film, usually a workprint, but it can be originals if no workprint is used.

FINE GRAIN—A description for the granularity of film stocks. Most slow ASA films have a finer grain quality than fast ASA films.

FLASHBACK—A cut in a film which goes back in time to a past event.

FLASHFORWARD—A cut in a film which goes forward in time to some future event.

FLASH FRAME—A clear or greatly overexposed frame (or frames) in a film which usually occurs between two shots in the film original. The flash frame (or frames) occurs as the camera slows down at the end of one shot and reaches speed at the beginning of the next.

FOCAL LENGTH—The optical length of a lens measured in millimeters. A variable focal length lens is a zoom lens.

FOCAL PLANE—The plane in the camera where a separate frame of film is exposed to light.

FOLLOW FOCUS—A technique used to keep a moving subject in focus for the duration of a shot. To follow focus, the focus setting on the lens must be changed during a shot to keep sharp focus on a moving subject which is coming closer to, or moving farther away from, the camera.

FORMAT—The gauge of film being used. Common formats are regular 8mm, Super-8, 16mm, 35mm and 70mm.

FULL COAT—A type of film, the same gauge as the format used for the visuals, which is fully coated with magnetic oxide and used as a sound medium for editing and double system playback/projection.

HIGH CONTRAST—In lighting, a type of lighting (low key) which has a range of bright areas and dark shadow areas and few grey areas. In film stocks, a high contrast film stock is a stock which responds primarily in terms of blacks and whites and not grey tones.

HIGH KEY—A type of lighting which is very bright and fully lit, with few shadow areas.

HOT SPOT—In a lighting setup, an area or portion of the set which is overly bright in relation to the rest of the set.

INPUT—In sound components, a jack or receptacle for jacking into a source or sources.

IPS—Means inches per second, and refers to the speed for record or playback on a tape or cassette recorder or player.

INTERLOCK—A double system playback set-up for film and sound in which the film projector and sound reproducer are synced mechanically or electronically.

JUMP CUT—A type of cut in which the two shots joined are discontinuous in terms of time and or space.

KEY LIGHT—The primary source of illumination for a subject.

LEADER—Filmstock which has no image (usually black, white or clear) which is used at the head and tail of a film. ACADEMY LEADER is numbered and used at the head of some film formats for changeover and syncing purposes.

LENS TURRET—A rotating device on some cameras which enables various lenses to be racked into position for filming. The turret usually holds fixed focus lenses, but can be used for a zoom lens and two prime lenses.

LIP SYNC—When spoken lines or dialogue are synchronized with film images. This can be accomplished in production through the use of single- or double-system synchronous systems or in post-production by dubbing.

LOW KEY—A type of lighting which is very dark and somber with a great many shadow areas.

MAGNETIC FILM—See FULL COAT.

MAGNETIC STRIPE—A magnetic oxide coating along the edge of the film. Used in single system filming-recording (newsfilm and Super-8), and in some instances for single-system sound projection.

MARRIED PRINT—A print of a film in which sound and visuals are united onto a single strand of film.

MATCH CUT—A type of cut in which the two shots joined are matched in terms of continuity.

MATTE BOX—A box or bellows device mounted in front of the taking lens. The matte box can be used as a sunshade or for special effects such as split screen, effects mattes, etc.

MIX—The blending of two or more sound sources onto a single track.

NEGATIVE—A film image in which all the tones or colors are the opposite of their true tone or color. Negative films are used in 16mm, 35mm, and 70mm filming.

NEW WAVE—The name given to a group of critics turned filmmakers in France in the early 1960s, specifically Truffaut, Godard, Chabrol, etc.

NORMAL LENS—A lens which accepts an angle of view similar to human perception—22–23 degrees. The focal length of this lens varies according to the format being used.

OPAQUE—Not transparent or translucent. In terms of film leader, black leader is opaque.

OPTICAL PRINTER—A printer which uses a lens for the printing of exposed stock onto raw stock. Usually used for blow-up or reduction from one format to another and for some special effects (freeze frame, split screen, etc.)

ORIGINAL—The footage shot in the camera.

OUTTAKE—Film workprint or original which is not used in the final edited version of the film.

OVEREXPOSURE—A shot which is too light because too much light was permitted to the film plane during exposure. Usually a result of improper f-stop setting.

OVER-THE-SHOULDER SHOT—A type of point of view shot which is taken over the shoulder of one actor relating to another.

PARALLAX—In non-reflex cameras, the difference between the viewing area of the taking lens and the viewing lens. Most non-reflex cameras have a parallax adjustment to correct this difference.

POSITIVE—A film image which has tones and colors rendered normally. The opposite of negative image.

POST-SYNCHRONIZATION—Adding any sound (dialogue, music, sound effects) during the editing of a film rather than recording these sounds while shooting.

PROCESSING—The developing of an exposed image by the lab.

QUARTZ LIGHT—A type of lamp for a lighting unit which is usually smaller, brighter, and longer lasting than a conventional tungsten light.

RAW STOCK—Unexposed footage.

REDUCTION—Done in an optical printer. An image on one format is reduced to a smaller format.

REFLEX VIEWING SYSTEM—A camera viewing system whereby the image coming through the lens and to the film plane is seen through the viewing system.

REVERSAL FILM—A film stock which after exposure and processing renders a positive image.

ROUGH CUT—The first edited version of a film. It is usually longer and less exact than the fine cut.

RUSHES—see DAILIES.

SET—The area or location which is being filmed.

SHOT—In filming, the length of time in which the camera is running, from camera start to camera off. In a film, a shot is the length of time between one cut and the next.

SINGLE FRAME—Recording film images one at a time rather than continuously. Usually accomplished with a cable release. See ANIMATION.

SLATE—In filming, the device used for marking shot numbers, takes, etc. at the beginning of the shot. Is usually used in sync sound shooting because the sound (the clap) and visual (the sticks coming together) can be synchronized. Also called CLAP BOARD.

SPLIT SCREEN—A projected image which is divided into two or more sections.

STORY BOARD—A pre-production step used for commercials and animated films in which hand-drawn frames representing shots or scenes are pasted in sequence on a large board. The story board is an aid in pre-production planning.

SWISH PAN—A very fast, usually blurry pan.

SYNCHRONIZATION—When sound track and picture run synchronously.

SYNCHRONIZER—A device used in editing to keep sound rolls and picture rolls in "sync."

TAKE—A camera shot. There can be several takes of a shot and the most successful one is used in the final film.

TELEPHOTO LENS—A lens which magnifies the image. Usually used for close-ups. Also called a long lens.

UNDEREXPOSURE—An image which is too dark, usually the result of an improper f-stop setting.

VARIABLE-SPEED MOTOR—A camera motor which is capable of a variety of transport speeds for fast and slow motion.

WASHED OUT—A shot which is over exposed.

WIDE ANGLE LENS—A lens which accepts a field of view wider than a normal lens. Usually used for long shots, establishing shots and for hand holding. Also called a short lens.

WIDE SCREEN—Any filming and projecting process which renders an image which is wider than the standard 1:33–1 ratio. Wide screen became popular in feature films in the ealy 1950s.

WORK PRINT—A contact printing copy of the camera original which is used for editing purposes.

ZOOM—In lenses, a variable focal length lens.

Index